Cambridge English

Compact
First

2nd edition

Teacher's Book

Peter May

CAMBRIDGE
UNIVERSITY PRESS

University Printing House, Cambridge CB2 8BS, United Kingdom

Cambridge University Press is part of the University of Cambridge.

It furthers the University's mission by disseminating knowledge in the pursuit of education, learning and research at the highest international levels of excellence.

www.cambridge.org
Information on this title: www.cambridge.org/9781107428577

© Cambridge University Press 2014

First published 2012
Reprinted 2015

Printed in the United Kingdom by Hobbs the Printer Ltd.

A catalogue record for this publication is available from the British Library

ISBN 978-1-107-42842-3 Student's Book without answers with CD-ROM
ISBN 978-1-107-42844-7 Student's Book with answers with CD-ROM
ISBN 978-1-107-42857-7 Teacher's Book
ISBN 978-1-107-42855-3 Workbook without answers with Audio
ISBN 978-1-107-42856-0 Workbook with answers with Audio
ISBN 978-1-107-42845-4 Student's Book Pack
ISBN 978-1-107-42848-5 Student's Pack
ISBN 978-1-107-42852-2 Class Audio CDs (2)

Contents

Map of the units

UNIT	TOPICS	GRAMMAR	VOCABULARY
1 Yourself and others	Daily life People	Review of present tenses Present simple in time clauses	Adjectives ending in -ed and -ing Character adjectives Forming adjectives: -able, -al, dis-, -ful, -ic, im-, -ish, -itive, -ive, -ous, un-, -y
2 Eating and meeting	Food and drink Restaurants Relationships	Review of past tenses	Fixed phrases
3 Getting away from it all	Travel and tourism Transport Festivals and customs	Review of modal verbs Adverbs of degree	Dependent prepositions
4 Taking time out	Entertainment (film, music, arts) Leisure	Verbs followed by to + infinitive or -ing too and enough Review of present perfect	Phrasal verbs with on
5 Learning and earning	Education, study and learning Careers and jobs	Review of future forms Countable and uncountable nouns	Phrasal verbs with take Noun suffixes: -or, -ist, -ian, -er, -ant
6 Getting better	Health and fitness Sport	Relative clauses (defining and non-defining) Purpose links	Medical vocabulary Phrasal verbs with up Sports vocabulary
7 Green issues	The environment The weather	Review of conditionals 1–3 Mixed conditionals Comparison of adjectives and adverbs Contrast links	Phrases with in
8 Sci & tech	Science Technology	Review of passive forms Articles	Communications vocabulary Science vocabulary Collocations
9 Fame and the media	The media Celebrities	Review of reported speech and reporting verbs	Media vocabulary Noun suffixes
10 Clothing and shopping	Shopping and consumer goods Fashion	Position of adverbs of manner and opinion Review of wish and if only Review of causative have and get	Clothing and shopping vocabulary Phrasal verbs with out Extreme adjectives

READING AND USE OF ENGLISH		WRITING	LISTENING	SPEAKING
Part 7: multiple matching	Part 3: word formation	Part 2 informal letter: getting ideas, informal language	Part 1: multiple-choice questions + short texts	Part 1: describing people, home
Part 6: gapped text	Part 2: open cloze	Part 2 article: linking expressions	Part 2: sentence completion	Part 2: giving opinions, comparing
Part 5: multiple-choice questions + long text	Part 1: multiple-choice cloze	Part 1 essay: linking expressions, for and against	Part 3: multiple matching	Part 3: turn taking, suggesting, speculating
Part 6: gapped text	Part 4: key word transformations	Part 2 review: descriptive adjectives, recommendations ·	Part 4: multiple-choice questions + long text	Part 4: asking for and justifying opinions
Part 7: multiple matching	Part 3: word formation	Part 2 formal letter of application: formal expressions, achieving aims	Part 2: sentence completion	Part 1: talking about future plans
Part 5: multiple-choice questions + long text	Part 2: open cloze	Part 2 letter: informal language, purpose links	Part 1: multiple-choice questions + short texts	Part 3: agreeing and politely disagreeing
Part 6: gapped text	Part 4: key word transformations	Part 1 essay: contrast links, for and against	Part 3: multiple matching	Part 2: comparing: *-er*, *more*, (*not*) *as … as*, etc.
Part 5: multiple-choice questions + long text	Part 1: multiple-choice cloze	Part 2 article: reason and result links, involving the reader	Part 2: sentence completion	Part 4: adding more points
Part 7: multiple matching	Part 3: word formation	Part 2 report: recommending and suggesting	Part 4: multiple-choice questions + long text	Part 2: keeping going
Part 6: gapped text	Part 4: key word transformations	Part 1 essay: extreme adjectives, for and against	Part 3: multiple matching	Parts 3 and 4: decision-making

Introduction

Who *Compact First Second Edition* is for

Compact First is a short but intensive final preparation course for students planning to take the *Cambridge English: First* exam, also known as *First Certificate of English (FCE)*. The course provides B2-level students with thorough preparation and practice of the grammar, vocabulary, language skills, topics and exam skills needed for success in all four papers of the exam: Reading and Use of English, Writing, Listening and Speaking. The course can be used by classes of any age, but it is particularly suitable for students over 17.

What the Student's Book contains

- *Compact First Second Edition* Student's Book has ten units for classroom use. Each unit covers all four papers, focusing on one part of each paper in each unit. The Reading and Listening texts cover all core *Cambridge English: First* topics. Writing tasks include both sample and model answers and follow a step-by-step approach. The Speaking activities are designed to improve fluency and accuracy, and to help students express themselves with confidence.

- Grammar pages provide additional focus on grammar and each unit ends with a revision page to check how well students have learned the grammar and vocabulary. The Vocabulary input is at B2 level and is based on English Vocabulary Profile. Grammar and vocabulary work is integrated in exam practice, including exercises based on research from the Cambridge Learner Corpus.

- *Quick steps* with advice on how to approach each part of all the exam papers.

- Exam tips with useful advice on exam strategies.

- Cross-references to the Writing, Listening and Speaking guides, and Grammar reference.

Writing, Listening and Speaking guides

These guides explain in detail what students can expect in Papers 2, 3 and 4, and give suggestions on how best to prepare and practise in each case. The guides include a summary of the strategies, advice and tips focused on in the units of the Student's Book with additional tasks and model answers in the Writing guide, and lists of useful expressions in the Speaking guide.

The **Grammar reference** gives clear explanations of all the main areas of grammar students need to know for *Cambridge English: First*.

Wordlist

The wordlist includes approximately 30 key words with definitions for each unit.

CD-ROM

The CD-ROM accompanying the Student's Book contains interactive exercises, including listening exercises that help students prepare for the exam, as well as an electronic version of the wordlist, and a link to the *Online Cambridge Advanced Learner's Dictionary*.

Student's Book with answers: this component includes all the answer keys and recording scripts for the Student's Book.

Other course components

Two Audio CDs: with listening material for the ten units of the Student's Book. The icon used with listening activities indicates the CD and track numbers.

Teacher's Book including:

- A list of aims for each unit.

- Step-by-step guidance for presenting and teaching all the material in the Student's Book. In some cases, alternative treatments and extension activities are suggested.

- Complete answer keys with recording scripts for both the Student's Book and Workbook. The keys include sample and model answers for Writing tasks.

- Five photocopiable progress tests, one for every two Student's Book units. The tests use a variety of non-exam task types.

Workbook without answers with Audio including:

- Ten units for homework and self-study corresponding to the Student's Book units. Each unit has four pages of exercises providing further practice and consolidation of the language and exam skills presented in the Student's Book. Exercises are based on research from the Cambridge Learner Corpus. Vocabulary is based on the English Vocabulary Profile.

- The Audio includes listening material for the Workbook.

Workbook with answers with Audio: this component includes all the answer keys and recording scripts for the Workbook.

Website

Two complete *Cambridge English: First* practice tests with accompanying audio as MP3 files are available on the website at www.cambridge.org/compactfirst.

Cambridge English: First

Overview

The *Cambridge English: First* examination has four papers.

Paper 1 Reading and Use of English 1 hour 15 minutes

Parts 1 and 3 mainly test your vocabulary; Part 2 mainly tests grammar. Part 4 often tests both. Answers are marked on a separate answer sheet.

Reading texts in Parts 5, 6 and 7 are about 550–650 words each. They are taken from newspaper and magazine articles, fiction, reports, advertisements, correspondence, messages and informational material such as brochures, guides or manuals. Answers are marked on a separate answer sheet.

Part	Task type	Questions	Format
1	Multiple choice gap-fill	8	You choose from words A, B, C or D to fill in each gap in a text.
2	Open gap-fill	8	You think of a word to fill in each gap in a text.
3	Word formation	8	You think of the right form of a given word to fill in each gap in a text.
4	Key word transformations	6	You complete a sentence with a given word so that it means the same as another sentence.
5	Multiple choice	6	You read a text followed by questions with four options: A, B, C or D.
6	Gapped text	6	You read a text with sentences removed, then fill in the gaps by choosing sentences from a jumbled list.
7	Multiple matching	10	You read 4–6 short texts and match the relevant sections to what the questions say.

Paper 2 Writing 1 hour 20 minutes

You have to do Part 1 plus **one** of the Part 2 tasks. In Part 2 you can choose one of questions 2–4. Answers are written in the booklet provided.

Part	Task type	Words	Format
1	Question 1 Essay	140–190	You write an essay giving your opinion on a given topic. You can use the ideas given and any of your own.
2	Questions 2–4 possible tasks: article, email/letter, report or review	140–190	You do a task based on a situation. The topic, reader and reason you are writing will be explained.

Paper 3 Listening about 40 minutes

You both hear and see the instructions for each task, and you hear all four parts twice.

If one person is speaking, you may hear information, news, instructions, a commentary, a documentary, a lecture, a message, a public announcement, a report, a speech, a talk or an advertisement. If two people are talking, you might hear a conversation, a discussion, an interview, part of a radio play, etc. Answers are marked on a separate answer sheet.

Part	Task type	Questions	Format
1	Multiple choice	8	You hear one or two people talking for about 30 seconds in eight different situations. For each question, you choose from answers A, B or C.
2	Sentence completion	10	You hear one person talking for about three minutes. For each question, you complete sentences by writing a word or short phrase.
3	Multiple matching	5	You hear five extracts, of about 30 seconds each, with a common theme. For each one, you choose from a list of six possible answers.
4	Multiple choice	7	You hear two people talking for about three minutes. For each question, you choose from answers A, B or C.

Paper 4 Speaking 14 minutes

You will probably do the Speaking test with one other candidate, though sometimes it is necessary to form groups of three. There will be two examiners, but one of them does not take part in the conversation.

Part	Task type	Minutes	Format
1	The examiner asks you some questions.	3–4	You talk about yourself.
2	You talk on your own for one minute.	3–4	You talk about two pictures and then comment on the other candidate's pictures.
3	You talk to the other candidate.	3–4	You discuss some prompts together.
4	You talk about things connected with the topic of Part 3.	3–4	You take part in a discussion with both the other candidate and the examiner.

Further information

For a full description of *Cambridge English: First*, including information about task types, testing focus and preparation for the exam, see the *Handbook*, which can be obtained from Cambridge English at: www.cambridgeenglish.org

1 Yourself and others

Unit objectives

TOPICS	daily life, people
GRAMMAR	review of present tenses, present simple in time clauses
VOCABULARY	adjectives ending in -ed and -ing, character adjectives, adjective prefixes and suffixes: -able, -al, dis-, -ful, -ic, im-, -ish, -itive, -ive, -ous, un-, -y
READING and USE OF ENGLISH	Part 7: studying an example item Part 3: word building, gist-reading, studying the example
WRITING	Part 2 informal letter: getting ideas, planning, checking
LISTENING	Part 1: studying an example script
SPEAKING	Part 1: asking for repetition, giving reasons and examples

Listening

Part 1

1 This activity could be done in pairs. Allow a few minutes' discussion time. Then ask students for their overall findings, and whether they think they have a good balance between work/study and relaxation.

Optional activity

Look at the exam task with the class. Make sure that students know what Part 1 consists of. You could ask the following questions. Encourage students to find the answers in the Listening guide on page 94 if they don't already know them.

1 How many extracts will you hear?

2 Is there any connection between the extracts?

3 Do you both read and hear the introductory sentence about each speaker and situation?

4 Do you both read and hear each question?

> **Answers**
> 1 eight   2 no   3 yes   4 no

2 Get students to study question 1, but not the transcript in Exercise 3. Check the answers.

> **Answers**
> 1 one male radio journalist reporting from the street
> 2 the focus is place

3 Explain to the class that multiple-choice questions in Listening (and Reading) often contain 'distractors' within the text that are designed to mislead them, and that in this task type there are always two distractors for each question. Allow time for students to talk about why C is right, and A and B are wrong, then elicit the answers.

Answers

C is the correct answer: *there isn't anybody in* means the people who live there are not at home, and *by the look of the place* indicates that the reporter is outside the house.

B is the wrong answer: the reporter says *away ... at a luxury hotel in the city centre*, so he is not there.

A is the wrong answer: he uses the conditional *would be* about someone else (the *TV crews*).

4 🔘 *1.02* Encourage pairs to look at the introductory sentence and question of each item, not the options. If they find it difficult to identify the focus, put the answers on the board in jumbled order. Go through the answers, and suggest that students ask themselves these questions every time they do Listening Part 1. Make sure that everyone reads and understands the Quick steps, then get students to work alone. Remind students to listen to the speakers' tone, as well as to the actual words they use. Play the recording through without pausing.

Answers

2 one female talking about travelling by train every day; focus: feelings/attitude

3 one female making a phone call; focus: purpose

4 one male talking about reading books at home; focus: reason

5 female and male (probably) talking in a holiday resort; focus: person

6 one male talking about staying healthy; focus: something he's doing

7 one female talking about where she lives; focus: place / type of home

8 female and male (probably) talking about finding something; focus: feelings

---

Recording script

You will hear people talking in eight different situations. For questions 1–8, choose the best answer (A, B or C).

1 *You hear a reporter talking on the radio.*

I'm standing here in Church Avenue with about thirty other media people, but <u>by the look of the place there isn't anybody in</u>. Nobody's quite sure if he'll be back later this afternoon – or whether he's spending the weekend away, perhaps at a luxury hotel in the city centre. What does seem clear, though, is that he's unlikely to play in Sunday's big match – otherwise these TV crews would be waiting at the gates of the club's training ground to film him, not here.

2 *You hear a woman talking about travelling to work every day.*

The traffic into town is getting worse all the time so the train was the obvious alternative. I'd kind of assumed I'd be able to sit back and relax with a newspaper and a cup of coffee, maybe chat with my fellow passengers and so on, but actually most mornings it's standing-room only with everyone squashed together, the conversation usually limited to 'excuse me'. Somebody is always pushing and you spend half your time trying to avoid falling over, so that <u>by the time you arrive you feel as though you've already done half a day's work</u>.

8   Unit 1   Yourself and others

3 You overhear a woman talking on the phone.

Well, I'm very sorry but <u>I'm just not prepared to pay for items I didn't receive</u>. As you say, I ordered the DVDs a fortnight ago, and when I did so I gave your sales department all the details they needed to deliver them to the right address, and it's not my fault if they sent them somewhere else. The only mistake I made was in dealing with your company in the first place. Next time I want things like that, I'll buy them online instead. Like most people do these days.

4 You hear a man talking about reading books.

I'm an editor in a publishing company and this month I'm working particularly hard on a rather long novel, so it may seem a little surprising that my favourite way of relaxing in the evenings is to sit down somewhere quiet with a good book. Whenever I can, I go into the study and settle down to read for as long as possible. <u>I just wish I could do so more often as I'm the kind of person who needs to get away from other people for a while</u>, but these days I'm usually just too busy helping out with the housework, and the kids.

5 You overhear a conversation in a holiday resort.

Man: The weather's been awful this summer, hasn't it? I'm not surprised people are looking so miserable. Those who haven't already gone home, that is. Non-stop rain spoils everything at the seaside.

Woman: I know. If I were a tourist I would've left too. The place is half-empty and <u>I've already had to reduce the number of staff</u>.

Man: Really? Is it that bad?

Woman: Yes, with so few customers <u>I just couldn't afford to keep paying their wages. I hated having to let them go</u>, especially as I used to be a waitress myself. But what else could I do?

Man: You had no choice. The same thing's happening everywhere round here.

6 You hear a man talking about staying healthy.

I was getting a bit worried about my unhealthy lifestyle, so I started spending a few hours each week at the local gym, but it was pretty boring and I haven't been for a while. Then someone suggested I should try <u>going to the office on foot</u> rather than taking the car, and I took her advice. I live a long way out in the suburbs and in fact I go right past the gym every day, but <u>it's really helping me get in shape</u>. And the funny thing is that with all this exercise I get more hungry and I'm actually having bigger meals now, but I'm told it doesn't matter because I'm using up a lot more energy.

7 You hear a woman talking about her home.

I'm staying at a friend's apartment downtown, but I'll move back into my place when they finish repainting it, probably on Friday. It's pleasant enough here, though I miss my garden with its beautiful bushes and trees. It's almost like being in the countryside there, even though <u>it's actually on the outskirts of town</u>. It's right on top of a hill, so from <u>my upstairs window</u> you can see the city-centre office buildings in one direction and a rural area not far away in the other. And a south-facing room gets lots of sunshine, too.

8 You overhear two people talking about finding something.

Woman: Yes, <u>it's just as well that memory stick turned up when it did. If it'd been missing any longer, I'd be getting a bit worried by now</u>.

Man: I knew it must be somewhere in the living room. If you remember, I suggested looking there the other day.

Woman: Actually, that wasn't where I found it.

Man: No? Where was it?

Woman: It was in the spare room, plugged into that old laptop of yours.

Man: Was it? Oh, I remember now, I was using it last year to copy some files. Sorry about that.

Woman: It doesn't matter now. Forget it.

Exam task answers

2A 3B 4B 5C 6C 7B 8B

5 Point out that candidates do not lose marks for incorrect answers, as this may not be the case in other exams they have taken. Allow 30 seconds for them to check, then go through the answers.

Grammar

Review of present tenses

1 This activity could be done in pairs. Give the class plenty of time to match the extracts, then check the answers. If you're teaching in the southern hemisphere, explain that 3 f seemed always true for the European who said it! Elicit or give more examples of each usage, and of stative verbs.

Answers

1c 2b 3f 4a 5g 6d 7e

2 Go through the answers when everyone has finished. If there is time, you may want to ask the class why they think each mistake has been made.

Answers

1 you understand   2 having fun   3 you like   4 'm/am waiting
5 I prefer   6 have   7 'm/am standing

3 This exercise practises all the uses presented in Exercise 1. If there is time, elicit these from the class, and ask which is a stative verb.

Answers

1 's/is writing (something happening right now)
2 are rising (a situation that is changing or developing)
3 quite often goes (a routine or habit)
4 are always shouting (something irritating or surprising)
5 belongs (stative verb)
6 'm/am staying (a temporary situation)
7 sets (something which is always true)
8 's/is having (something happening right now)

Present simple in time clauses

4 The students' first language may use a future form in these clauses, so it's important they realise that in these extracts we are using the present simple with future meaning, as in first conditional forms. Elicit the answers and then some more examples with a variety of time expressions such as *before*, *after* or *until*.

Answers

yes, present simple

5 Give students a little time to study the sentences, then go through the answers.

Answers

1 'll get, go   2 I'll wait, come   3 ends, 'll catch   4 won't, start
5 arrive, 'll be   6 'll talk, get

6 Allow a minute or two for students working on their own to write their answers, then get them to work in pairs. Elicit some answers for each question.

Suggested answers

1 I get home.   2 I go on holiday.   3 I have enough money.
4 I'm thirty.   5 I pass Proficiency.   6 I finish my homework.

Reading and Use of English

Reading Part 7

1 This activity could be done in pairs. Allow plenty of time for discussion of the daily lives of the people in the photos. The four people talk about their lives in the Reading text, but don't mention this yet – it will give students an extra reason for reading later on.

2 Give the class a minute or two to look at the instructions, the prompt *Which person*, the question numbers and the text layout. Then check the answers.

Answers

1 four   2 one text in four sections   3 four people's daily lives
4 which person does or thinks particular things
5 ten   6 yes

3 Give students two or three minutes to skim the text for the answers to the two questions. Then check the answers.

Answers

1 B Assistant Sales Manager
2 A University student
3 C Website Designer
4 D Tour Guide
earliest B, latest C

4 Explain that in many cases, there are 'distractors' – words or sentences in the text which appear to give the right answer if they are not read carefully. This activity raises awareness of how distractors work. Go through the answers once students have had enough time to study the three highlighted parts.

Answers

B: Correct – if lunch is the first meal of the day for her, she can't have eaten breakfast.
A: If there's time he has tea and toast, so it's not true to say he never has breakfast.
D: Usually she skips (misses) breakfast, but not always – she sometimes has 'cereal or something'.

5 Make sure that everyone studies the Exam tip and answer any questions about this. Then give students about 20 minutes to do the multiple-matching task on their own, in exam conditions. If you don't want them to underline in the book, tell them to note down the first few words of each relevant phrase or sentence. Go through the answers, and elicit the relevant phrases and sentences. If there is time, also elicit some of the distractors, e.g. A's reference to missing the train relates to the past, not the present (7).

Exam task answers

1 C   2 A   3 C   4 B   5 A   6 D   7 A   8 B   9 D   10 B

Underlining

A

(5)   'Assuming I don't oversleep, which can happen
(7)   I do the uphill walk into town, which wakes me up and enables me to plan what I'm going to do in the morning and afternoon
(2)   I sometimes head for the gym, but not as often as I should

B

(4)   a dash to the station to catch the 7.15
(10) dealing with client queries, which for me is one of the most interesting, challenging and worthwhile aspects of the job
(8)   At first I found working here pretty stressful, but I'm used to it now and it doesn't bother me.

C

(3)   the previous evening. 'If I have a creative peak,' he says, 'that's when it is
(1)   having a 20-minute lie-down after lunch. Then, when I wake up

D

(9)   It's the custom here to have a sleep after lunch, but I haven't got time for that. In any case, I'm not tired then
(6)   can be a bit irritating if I end up doing unpaid overtime

Adjectives ending in *-ed* and *-ing*

6 Give students time to study the context of each word and work out the rules. If necessary, explain the meaning of the B2-level words (*exhausted, fascinating, challenging, refreshed, distracted, irritating*) as listed by English Profile. Check the answers and elicit the corresponding *-ed/-ing* adjective for each of the eight words, then elicit further examples such as *amazed/amazing* and *bored/boring*.

Answers

1 -ed   2 -ing

7 Point out that this exercise is partly a preparation for Word Formation in Reading and Use of English later in this unit, and that spelling is important, e.g. dropping the final *e* in some cases. Both parts of the exercise could be done individually or in pairs. Encourage brief answers to the questions, using the words given. Check answers to the sentence-completion part of the exercise, and elicit some answers to the questions. Also elicit the other form of each adjective.

Note: one of the forms of all eight adjectives is listed as B2 level by English Profile.

Answers

1 relaxed   2 amusing   3 worried   4 depressing   5 motivated
6 terrified   7 astonishing   8 puzzling

8 Where possible, students should work with others they don't know very well, using the prompts from Exercise 7 and as many -ing/-ed adjectives as they can.

Speaking

Part 1

Optional activity

Make sure that students know what Part 1 consists of. You could ask the following questions. Encourage students to find the answers in the Speaking guide on page 97 if they don't already know them.

1   How many examiners are there?

2   Do you answer questions from just one examiner?

3   How many candidates are there?

4   Do you talk to the other candidate(s) in Part 1?

Answers

1 two   2 yes   3 usually two, but occasionally there may be
three   4 no

1 Explain that in the exam students may be asked questions about future plans and ambitions, and that these will be practised in Unit 5. You may also want to point out that candidates are always asked the first two questions here, while the others are taken from lists that examiners may choose from.

Answers

1 your town
2 what you like about your town
3 your family
4 your favourite season, and why
5 what you like doing on holiday
6 what you use the Internet for
(all questions are about you)
You would use the present simple to reply, although in some cases you may also need to use the present continuous, for example to say a relative is studying abroad.

2 Focus attention on the Exam tip before students start this activity, and perhaps mention that the two mistakes are both incorrect uses of verb tenses. Allow time for pairs to work on this, then elicit the answers.

Suggested answers

1 One-word answer. He gives examples when asked *in what ways*, but he could have done this without being prompted.
2 The verb form should be *I stay*.
3 She doesn't give a reason. She could reply as she does after the examiner asks *why* without being prompted.
4 The verb form should be *I go*.
5 Not polite. He could say *Could you repeat that, please?*
6 He doesn't give a reason for not liking newspapers. He could say something like *because there's too much in them about politics* or *I listen to the radio news, so I don't need to.*

3 Students should be familiar with all the basic frequency adverbs like *usually*, and aware that these normally go before the main verb. Elicit the answer to the first question, then tell the class to look at the six expressions and answer the questions. Go through the answers, and elicit more examples such as *twice a month* and *every few minutes*. Point out that *hardly ever* is quite often tested in Reading and Use of English and other parts of the exam.

Answers

1 at the end (*hardly ever* goes before the verb)
2 hardly ever
3 from time to time / now and then

4 If possible get everyone to sit with somebody they don't know very well: this activity can be a useful ice-breaker. Monitor pairs and feed in language where necessary.

5 Tell pairs to be polite and constructive in their comments about each other's speaking. Allow a minute for this, and then elicit some comments on the students' own performance (not on their partners' speaking), and note any particular difficulties.

Character adjectives

6 Point out that this is a light-hearted activity with no 'right' or 'wrong' answers – or 'key' purporting to analyse their personality. Give students a couple of minutes each to answer.

7 These adjectives are all B2 level as shown by English Profile. Encourage the use of dictionaries if students have any difficulties, then check that everyone has the right answers. They then compare their impressions of each other using some of the adjectives. Advise students to be careful not to upset their partners, avoiding answers such as *always bossy*, even if it's true! Monitor pairs to make sure that they do so, and to avoid possible embarrassment don't elicit answers when everyone has finished. Finally, students use modals such as *could*, *might* and *may* to speculate about the character of the people in the photos. Elicit some answers, and point out that the language used in this activity is useful practice for Writing later in this unit.

Answers

1 thoughtful   2 optimistic   3 childish   4 bossy   5 practical
6 impatient   7 ambitious   8 sensitive   9 decisive
10 unpredictable   11 reasonable   12 disorganised

Reading and Use of English

Forming adjectives

1 Get students to note down the words and then underline them if you don't want them to write in the book. Make sure that everyone has the right answers. You may want to elicit the base words, e.g. *ambition*, *boss*, etc., pointing out that some are nouns but others are verbs and adjectives.

Answers

reasonable (*also* unpredictable), practical, disorganised, thoughtful, optimistic, impatient, childish, sensitive, decisive, ambitious, unpredictable, bossy

2 Elicit that when adding a suffix beginning with a vowel, we drop the final *e*, e.g. *adventure – adventurous*. Encourage the use of dictionaries to find antonyms and check spelling.

Remind students to add both a prefix and suffix, e.g. *unadventurous*, where possible. Then elicit all the answers, possibly putting them on the board or OHP. Elicit more adjectives (not necessarily of character) with each of these prefixes and suffixes, plus their meanings and possibly also their opposites.

Answers

(un)adventurous, aggressive, anxious, artistic, cautious, cheeky, competitive, (un)emotional, energetic, (un)enthusiastic, foolish, greedy, (un)helpful, dishonest, pessimistic, impolite, unpopular, (un)reliable, (dis)respectful, (un)sympathetic

Optional activity

Encourage discussion about whether some of these adjectives describe positive or negative characteristics, pointing out that in certain cases, e.g. *pessimistic*, *cautious*, the answers are subjective. Elicit answers from the class, making sure that all the words are understood.

Suggested answers

'good' – *artistic, energetic, enthusiastic, helpful, honest, polite, reliable, sympathetic*
'bad' – opposites of the above (*unenthusiastic, unhelpful, unreliable, unsympathetic*), plus *aggressive, cheeky, foolish, greedy, dishonest, impolite, unpopular*
'good' or 'bad' – *adventurous, anxious, cautious, competitive, emotional, pessimistic* and *respectful* could be positive or negative in certain circumstances

Part 3

3 Explain that all the mistakes in these sentences involve prefixes and suffixes students have studied in this unit, though in most cases with different adjectives. Elicit answers when they have finished. You may want to ask what students think the most common mistakes are by speakers of their first language(s).

Answers

1 charming   2 impolite   3 healthy   4 disorganised   5 sociable
6 stressful

4 Like Exercise 1, this exercise focuses on prefixes and suffixes studied in this unit. Students have also seen all the base words, although they will have to be careful which form to choose as two or three prefixes and/or suffixes may be possible. Explain that this is in effect a sentence-level version of Word Formation, although of course in the exam it is unlikely that all the target words would be adjectives requiring prefixes and suffixes. Go through the answers once students have finished, highlighting spelling.

Answers

1 optimistic   2 challenging   3 depressed   4 unsympathetic
5 refreshed   6 unenthusiastic

5 Tell the class to read the instructions carefully and look very quickly at the way the text and the words in capitals are laid out. Then go through the answers.

Answers

1 eight
2 a word formed from the word in capitals at the end of the same line
3 mainly vocabulary (especially prefixes and suffixes)

6 Set a time limit for this of no more than a minute, and advise students to do this every time they do a Word Formation task. Explain that some answers may require an understanding of more than one sentence, or the text as a whole. Check the answers and deal with any comprehension difficulties that relate to the gist of the text, but not the detail.

Answers

The purpose of the text is to show how different people from the same family can be.
paragraph 1: to introduce the topic
paragraph 2: to describe one of the daughters
paragraph 3: to describe the other daughter
paragraph 4: to describe the son

7 Explain that students should look at the example and its context every time they begin a Word Formation task, as this will give them an introduction to the text, and also remind them of what they must do in this task type. Go through the answers with the class.

Answers

1 an adjective   2 what causes a feeling (to friends of the family)
3 *-ing*   4 drop the final *e*

Point out that students have already seen some form or other of all the target words in this exam task. You may also want to give some clues or further tips before they begin - for instance, the need to watch out for plural forms. Allow ten to twelve minutes for students working on their own to fill in or note down their answers. Remind them to make sure they have changed all the words in capital letters. Then check answers. Elicit the prefixes and suffixes used, and highlight the use of two of these in question 4. Pay particular attention to spelling in 1, 5, 6, 7 and 8.

Exam task answers

1 personalities   2 motivated   3 ambitious   4 unemotional
5 sensitive   6 sympathetic   7 adventurous   8 anxious

Writing

Part 2 informal letter

1 When the class has had time to look at the exam task, elicit the answers.

> **Answers**
>
> 1 an English friend / Alex
> 2 write back saying: how important friends are to you, who your best friend is, what you like about him or her
> 3 informal
>   a *I've, don't, I'd, Who's*; b *kid, do*; c *So, and*;
>   d exclamation mark; e *Looking forward to hearing from you*

2 Give students a few minutes to read the model answer and answer the questions. Elicit the answers.

> **Answers**
>
> 1 yes
> 2 no
> 3 Dear Alex, Best wishes
> 4 Introduction: she thanks Alex for his/her message and comments on this.
>   Conclusion: she talks about the future and asks Alex to write back soon and give her more information.
> 5 Yes: the importance of friends in the first main paragraph, who her best friend is in the second main paragraph, a description of her friend's personality in the third main paragraph.
> 6 Informal expressions such as *thanks, just down the road, mates, a bit*; dash and exclamation marks; contracted forms: *they're, who's, we've, she's*; linkers: *and, but*; friendly expressions: *It was great to hear from you, Write soon*
> 7 *indecisive, practical, bossy, thoughtful, sympathetic*
> 8 *tell each other, can be ... at times, whenever I ... she's always, cheer me up, sense of humour, have the chance*, etc.

3 Refer the class to the instructions in the exam task, and to the Exam tip. This is very much a personal task and best done individually – point out there are no 'right' or 'wrong' answers to these questions, either. Monitor students' work and make suggestions where necessary, especially for question 1, but don't elicit answers.

4 Get students to make their plan quickly, using very brief notes.

5 Give the class no more than 40 minutes to write their answers, as that is what they will have in the exam and they have already studied the task and planned their work. Tell students always to leave at least five minutes at the end of each Writing task to check their work, and to refer back to these five points in future units and other Part 1 and Part 2 tasks. Checking could be done as a peer correction activity, although of course this will not be possible in the exam itself.

Model answer

Hi Alex,

It's always great to hear from you!

You're absolutely right about how much friendship matters. Life just wouldn't be the same if we didn't have friends, would it?

My very best friend is called Luis and we've grown up together, really. We first met at primary school and he's been my best mate ever since.

We're quite similar in a lot of ways. For instance, we're the same age, almost exactly the same height and weight, and we're both crazy about sports, especially basketball and swimming.

Like me, he can be rather shy at times, though he's perhaps a little more talkative than me. He's also someone you can rely on to help you if you're in trouble or worried about something. He's a fantastic friend and I'm sure you'd get on really well with him.

Hope to hear from you again soon!

Bye for now,

Enrique

Revision

1 | **Answers**

> 1 'm/am staying, 'm/am working
> 2 usually eat, 're/are having
> 3 'm/am waiting, seems
> 4 is changing, are getting
> 5 is, 's/is always complaining
> 6 own, don't live
> 7 gets, 'm/am thinking

2 | **Answers**

> 1 greedy 2 dishonest 3 artistic 4 impolite 5 energetic
> 6 cautious 7 pessimistic

3 | **Answers**

> 1 unpredictable 2 sympathetic 3 unreasonable
> 4 challenging 5 thoughtful 6 decisive

4 | **Answers**

> 1 relaxing 2 reliable 3 practical 4 terrifying
> 5 astonished 6 aggressive 7 competitive 8 childish
> 9 puzzling 10 exhausted

Remind students that there is more practice on the CD-ROM.

2 Eating and meeting

Unit objectives

TOPICS	food and drink, restaurants, relationships
GRAMMAR	review of past tenses
VOCABULARY	fixed phrases
READING and USE OF ENGLISH	Part 6: studying an example item Part 2: fixed phrases, auxiliary verbs
WRITING	Part 2 article: narrative linking expressions
LISTENING	Part 2: identifying the kind of words needed
SPEAKING	Part 2: comparing pictures, expressing opinions

Reading and Use of English

Part 6

1 This activity could be done in pairs. Explain that in some countries most students go to a university away from their home town. Be ready to help out with food vocabulary, and with the names for objects in question 3. The words given as examples appear later in the Reading text.

2 Give students a couple of minutes to look at the task, then elicit the answers.

> **Answers**
> 1 an article with six sentences removed
> 2 the missing sentences
> 3 no – only six of them

3 Allow no more than two minutes for these gist questions, then elicit the answers.

> **Answers**
> 1 He was feeling unhealthy.
> 2 He began to feel better and his appearance improved

4 Get the class to read just the first two paragraphs, deal with any language difficulties students may have, and then tell them to look at sentence C only. In pairs, they decide what kind of links the underlined expressions provide, e.g. contrast. Elicit the answers and ask if there are any other links, e.g. *I was more concerned with / might be important after all* (contrast), *Especially as* (another reason).

> **Answers**
> *At that time* and *Before long* are time links (see Writing in this unit) that in this case indicate a progression. The use of *though* shows there is a contrast in meaning, *those* refers back to *ready meals,* and *cooking for myself* contrasts with *heat up ready meals.*
> C couldn't fit gap 2 because *those* is plural and *(junk) food* is uncountable. It would not make any sense referring to *meals.*

5 Allow 20 minutes at most for students to do the exam task, working individually. If you don't want them to write in the book, get them to note down the words in the text and the sentences which are linked to each other.

> **Exam task answers**
> 2 F 3 G 4 E 5 B 6 A

> **Answers**
> 2 At first / But after a few months, I couldn't believe / realise it was true, unhealthy appearance / in bad shape
> 3 I took time ... / In the same way, I got to know the best times to ... when to / These changes
> 4 But / On the more positive side, took some reorganising and a commitment to set aside time / doing all this
> 5 throw the whole thing in the oven / Cooking it that way, fish or chicken portions ... vegetables / tasty meal
> 6 I'd let ... abandoned / I hadn't (past perfect: see Grammar in this unit)

6 Give the class a minute to make sure they have answered every question, then check the answers to the exam task and elicit the expressions that link gaps 1–6 with sentences A–G.

7 Give students plenty of time to find the words and phrases, then go through the answers, eliciting more examples using each expression.

> **Answers**
> 1 heat up   2 snacking   3 junk food   4 skipping meals
> 5 living on   6 balanced diet   7 portions   8 starving
> 9 filling   10 pick up a bargain

Listening

Part 2

1 Divide the class into pairs. Explain that they will hear some of these words and expressions on the recording, but don't say which words and expressions at this stage. (They are: *delicious, dish, catering, vegetarian, ingredients.*) Also point out that *dish* means 'part of a meal' here, that *go off* in this context means 'go bad', that students should use *chop* and *slice* as verbs, and that *tough* can be applied to steak, for example, or to other nouns such as *work* (as on the recording). Answer any questions students may have about any of the other expressions in the list, then allow a few minutes for them to talk about the photo, which is linked to the theme of the Part 2 recording.

Optional activity

Look at the exam task with the class. Make sure that students know what Part 2 consists of. You could ask the following questions. Encourage students to find the answers in the Listening guide on page 95 if they don't already know them.

1   What kind of extract will you hear?

2   How many speakers?

3   How do you give your answers?

When the class has had time to read the exam instructions, elicit the answers and answer any more questions about this task type that students may have.

2 🔘 *1.03* For item 1, elicit possible words: *mother*, *father*, *friend*, *partner*, etc. so that students can compare their answer to what is on the recording when they hear it. This activity could be done in pairs. Point out that for some answers in item 2 there may be more than one possibility.

Suggested answers

1 noun, probably a person; a close relationship, perhaps a relative or friend
2 2 noun   3 date   4 noun (phrase)   5 noun (phrase)
6 noun   7 adjective   8 noun (phrase)   9 adverb   10 noun

Make sure that the class read and understand the Exam tip, then get them to work on their own. Play the recording through without pausing.

Recording script

You will hear a restaurant chef talking about his work. For questions 1–10, complete the sentences.

Max

It's difficult to say when exactly I made up my mind I wanted to cook for a living, because I'd always been interested in cooking. As a child I used to watch my parents preparing meals at home, and I would imagine myself cooking something delicious for the family. But (1) <u>it wasn't until my elder sister showed me how to create some really original dishes that I realised I wanted to make a career of it.</u> Though she wasn't a chef and in fact I very nearly wasn't either because my dad had other ideas.

He was an engineer but in his younger days he would've loved to be (2) <u>a footballer, so when he saw I could play a bit he tried to persuade me to take it up professionally and forget about cooking.</u> But by then I knew I was better with a frying pan than a ball, and I didn't take any notice.

It would be a while before I actually began work, though. First I went to catering college, in the autumn of 1999, and studied there until (3) <u>2001. Towards the end of that year I was offered work at a hotel in London, and I accepted straightaway.</u> That job was tough at first, extremely tough. I was working very long hours when I was there and it was always unbelievably hot in the kitchens, but (4) <u>it was the head chef who really got me down. He treated us like slaves, and I hated him so much I hardly noticed the working conditions.</u> As soon as I could, I moved to France.

Some people were surprised by my decision to do that, but I'd been thinking of going to Paris for some time before I actually went. And although I hardly knew any of the language (5) <u>I had a very useful contact there: the owner of one of the city's top restaurants. I'd met him</u> when he was staying at the hotel in London, and fortunately he was very impressed by the meal I'd made for him. And the rest, as they say, is history.

I worked there for five years, developing my skills and sometimes preparing dishes for celebrities. (6) <u>They included film stars,</u> unlike at the London hotel where they tended to be big-name sportspeople, or rock stars.

Nowadays I have a restaurant of my own, and our regular customers also include quite a few well-known faces. It's popular with people from both home and abroad, and I have a team of four chefs from different countries. Even so, (7) <u>I try to ensure, wherever possible, that all our vegetables, fruit and meat comes from local farms.</u> It gives them business, and it makes environmental sense, too. In terms of the cooking, I suppose what makes it special is (8) <u>the variety of dishes on the menu, actually, rather than any one type such as vegetarian or fish dishes. That's what I really take pride in,</u> because it's not something that's easy to achieve.

Unlike in many other restaurants, we only cook when we receive orders from (9) <u>customers. So to ensure that their food is freshly made, we need to keep all the ingredients ready for anything they might choose</u> from the menu. And that's difficult because there are so many things that can go wrong. Starting with deliveries. They can turn up late, as the meat did on Friday, or even disappear altogether, which is what happened to (10) <u>a van heading here last July. I still wonder what the thieves did with several hundred kilos of fish</u> at the hottest time of the year.

Exam task answers

1 (elder) sister   2 a (professional) footballer   3 2001
4 head chef   5 restaurant owner   6 film/movie stars   7 local
8 variety   9 freshly   10 fish

3 Give everyone a couple of minutes to check for accuracy in their writing, then go through the answers. With a strong class, you may want to ask what makes the speakers laugh at the end: the two meanings of *catch* (possibly similar in the students' first language), and the literal and metaphorical meanings of *slip through the net* (there may also be a similar first language-expression).

Giving your opinion

4 This activity could be done in pairs. It lets students discuss the topic of the recording, and also introduces language they can use in Speaking. Give them a couple of minutes to talk about Max's job, then move on.

Grammar

Review of past tenses

1 This activity could be done in pairs. Students should be familiar with all these past tense forms, but they may not be so clear how to use them, or what the forms indicate. Elicit the names of the tenses. Then give students time to match the examples and uses. Check the answers and then elicit more examples of each past tense form, particularly *used to* and *would*, e.g. *They used to see each other every Friday evening and they would go dancing together.*

Answers

1 d past simple   2 e past continuous   3 a past perfect
4 f past perfect continuous   5 b *used to / didn't use to*
6 c *would*

2 Encourage students to look at the rules in Exercise 1 while they correct the sentences. Check the answers, asking why the sentences are wrong.

Answers

1 he'd / he had left his bike
2 Anita was crying
3 we'd / we had organised *or* we'd / we had been organising for weeks
4 I was a member
5 the house had been empty
6 someone was walking
7 people didn't use to worry
8 because I'd / I had decided

3 Be ready to help out with any new vocabulary, e.g. *adopt*, *widow*, while students complete the sentences, but first let them try to work out the meanings from context. Go through the answers. If there is time, ask why the other options are wrong.

Answers

1 C   2 A   3 B   4 C   5 B   6 C

4 Explain any new vocabulary, such as *stepbrother*. Allow a minute or two for students working on their own to write their answers. When everyone has finished, check their work for accuracy. Elicit some answers from the class.

Suggested answers

1 was walking along the road.
2 used to go away with my family.
3 had been crying.
4 was doing a summer job.
5 would play lots of games.
6 had gone home.

Speaking

Part 2

1 Students study the sentences, filling in the numbered gaps. Warn them to be careful with grammatical constraints, and point out that the words they choose in sentences d and g must make sense for both gaps, e.g. 4 can't be *difference* because 5 must be *both*. Go through the answers.

Note: some contrast links other than *but* could be highlighted here, but these will covered in Speaking Part 2 in Unit 7.

Answers

2 other   3 similar   4 similarity   5 both   6 same   7 both
8 different   9 difference   10 other

2 This activity could be done in pairs. Tell students to look quickly at points a–f, without going into any detail at this stage. Tell them not to treat this as an exam task yet. Elicit one-word answers only to each of points a–f.

Answers

a different   b different   c same   d similar   e different
f different

3 Pairs repeat Exercise 2, but using the second set of photos and without prompts. As in the exam, they have to find the similarities and differences for themselves. Give them a couple of minutes, then elicit some of the points, but not the actual similarities and differences.

4 Tell students to ignore the photos for the moment. Remind them that occasionally there are three candidates, but the usual number is two. Check that everyone has the correct answers, and suggest that they ask themselves these questions whenever they practise Speaking Part 2.

Answers

Photographs 1 and 2
A Talk for a minute, comparing their two photos. Say what they think could be enjoyable about having a meal there.
B Say whether they like to eat in restaurants.
Photographs 3 and 4
B Talk for a minute, comparing their two photos. Say why they think people choose to eat there.
A Say which of the two kinds of place they prefer to go to.

5 For the exam task, focus attention on the Quick steps, as the first two points bring together the work students have done in *Giving your opinion* (on Student's Book page 18) and in Exercises 1, 2 and 3. For photographs 1 and 2, suggest that Candidate B keep an eye on the time so that A is not constantly checking their watch to see if the minute is up! Point out that B should spend about 20 seconds answering their question, giving a reason or example. Monitor pairs as they discuss both sets of photos, ensuring that the non-speaker does not interrupt their partner and that the speaker doesn't go on too long.

6 Students change roles so that they both have had a chance to discuss the other pair of photos. Encourage them to vary the language used, not copy what their partner said.

7 Remind pairs to be polite and constructive in their comments. Allow a minute or two, and then elicit some comments on the students' own performance (not on their partners' speaking), and note any particular difficulties, such as keeping going for a full minute.

Reading and Use of English

Fixed phrases

1 This activity could be done in pairs. You may want to explain some of the more difficult phrases before students begin, but point out that there are contextual clues to help them, including grammatical constraints. Check the answers and elicit some examples, e.g. *What makes you feel at ease? What gets on your nerves? When do you want people to keep you company? When do you want people to leave you alone?*

Answers

1 at ease   2 get on my nerves   3 lose touch   4 at first sight
5 is attracted to   6 propose to her   7 leave me alone
8 keep me company   9 break my heart
10 takes me for granted

Part 2

2 Give the class a minute to look at the instructions and task, then elicit the answers. Contrast this task with Reading and Use of English Part 6, where whole sentences are missing but are given in jumbled order.

Answers

1 eight   2 one   3 no – you must think of them for yourself

3 Allow only a minute or so for students to answer the questions, and then elicit the answers. Then give students, working on their own, no more than 15 minutes to complete the exam task. Point out that some of the items focus on expressions presented in Exercise 1, and others on past tenses.

Answers

1 The title means 'a formal agreement to a marriage; the agreement did not last long'. In the last paragraph it is clear that Emily ended that agreement.
2 an extract from a biography or biographical article

Exam task answers

1 those   2 first   3 to   4 had   5 getting   6 at   7 taking   8 off

4 Give the class a minute to check that they have put a word for every question, then go through the answers, also eliciting the meanings of topic-related expressions that may be new to the class, such as *engaged/engagement*, *break off* and *son-in-law*.

Answers

fixed phrases: 2, 3, 5, 6, 7; past tenses: 0, 4

Writing

Linking expressions

1 This activity could be done in pairs. The B2-level linking expressions may be new to the class, so let students use their dictionaries if they find them difficult. Go through the answers, eliciting another example with each expression, and suggest that students try to incorporate some of them into their story writing and speaking.

Answers

1 at first   2 between those two times   3 as soon as
4 very surprisingly   5 immediately   6 at the same time

Part 2 article

2 When the class has had time to look at the exam task, elicit the answers.

Answers

1 young people who read an international website
2 the past
3 140–190

3 Give students a few minutes to read the model answer and answer the questions. Elicit the answers.

Answers

1 yes
2 Neutral. Although the model answer uses some informal features such as conversational expressions to address the reader, words such as *fun*, *kid* and *sure*, and exclamation marks, there are no contracted forms and it is written in complete sentences, some of them quite complex.
3 The mystery of who is at the door arouses their curiosity / creates suspense.
4 The person who sent the text was someone mentioned in the previous paragraph.
5 I sat at home watching TV, how delighted I was, meeting people, invited me out for dinner

4 Give students plenty of time to find the examples and expressions. For item 1, refer the class to the third Quick step and perhaps elicit more examples. Item 2 provides examples in context of the target grammar in this unit, and item 3 presents new expressions. You may also want to highlight the use in the text of lower-level linkers such as *first*, *after that* and *then*. Go through the answers with the class; if time allows, elicit more examples with the linking expressions, and elicit the meanings of any expressions students may be unsure about, e.g. *for once* = something happened that doesn't usually happen.

Answers

1 Have you ever felt, You can imagine, I think you will agree
2 past continuous: *was going*; past perfect: *had given*, *had been*; past perfect continuous: *had been talking*
3 a the moment   b before long   c eventually

5 Tell the class they can use linking expressions from the text, but apart from that they must write a completely different article. Encourage them to think of a situation and series of events that will interest readers. Allow about 40 minutes for this task, including time to check at the end, using the points in Unit 1 Writing Exercise 5.

Model answer

Out at night

I've had several great nights out in my life, but one that sticks in my memory is when I did actually have a great night out – and I mean out!

I was sixteen years old. My parents couldn't afford holidays abroad, so they encouraged me to go camping overnight with three friends. I'd never been camping before and we immediately got off to a bad start. We couldn't read a map, so we lost our way. Then my feet began to hurt, so we arrived late and in the dark at the place where we had decided to camp.

You might think that the whole trip was a disaster but as soon as we put the tents up, things changed. We cooked a meal on our stove and made a hot drink. Then Lorenzo got out his guitar and we started singing. Can you imagine singing 'Starry Starry Night', lying on your back and looking at the stars above you? We never got into our sleeping bags. It was a great night out!

Revision

1 | **Answers**

1 was eating   2 had arranged   3 used to go   4 would spend   5 went   6 met   7 gave   8 'd been waiting   9 was starting   10 'd sent   11 'd forgotten   12 did   13 suggested   14 'd given up   15 ran

2 | **Answers**

1 at first sight   2 I lost touch   3 at ease   4 keep you company   5 Josef's heart   6 take you for granted   7 it gets on my nerves   8 leave me alone

3 | **Answers**

1 Eventually   2 meantime   3 Once   4 moment   5 long   6 amazement

4 | **Answers**

Across
5 dish   6 filling   8 propose   9 skip   14 tough   15 portion   16 consume
Down
1 slice   2 adopt   3 chop   4 snack   7 ripe   9 starving   10 widow   11 bargain   12 divorce   13 junk

Remind students that there is more practice on the CD-ROM.

3 Getting away from it all

Unit objectives

TOPICS	travel and tourism, transport, festivals and customs
GRAMMAR	review of modal verbs, adverbs of degree
VOCABULARY	dependent prepositions
READING and	Part 5: focusing on an example item, writer's purpose
USE OF ENGLISH	Part 1: dependent prepositions
WRITING	Part 1 essay: linking expressions, for and against
LISTENING	Part 3: focusing on key words, predicting content
SPEAKING	Part 3: suggesting, speculating, turn-taking

Listening

Part 3

1 Allow the use of dictionaries for this matching activity, and/ or give definitions where necessary. Encourage discussion of shades of meaning, such as a *trip* tending to take less time than a *journey*, *to cruise* possibly indicating a more leisurely voyage than *to sail*. Also elicit or introduce collocations like *pony trekking* and *river cruise*. Go through the answers, possibly eliciting more nouns that are used with *to go* and *to go on*.

> **Answers**
>
> to: cruise, explore, tour, wander
> to go: hitchhiking, sailing, sightseeing, trekking
> to go on a/an: cruise, expedition, flight, tour, trip, voyage

Optional activity

Students often make mistakes with the word *travel*, possibly as a result of first-language interference.

Read aloud these five sentences and ask students to replace the word *travel* where necessary.

1 Air travel is becoming more and more expensive.
2 She works in the travel industry.
3 It's a long travel to Alaska.
4 I read about his travels in Africa.
5 Enjoy your travel to Italy.

Go through the answers quickly, and elicit more examples of correct use, e.g. *travel agent*, *air travel*, *back from her travels*.

> **Suggested answers**
>
> 3 It's a long journey to Alaska. (*or* voyage)
> 5 Enjoy your trip to Italy.

2 This activity could be done in pairs. Make sure that everyone knows what each place in the list is, then ask students to name the places in the photos. They will hear about these places on the recording. Get pairs to discuss the five photos briefly. Remind the class that there are no

photos in the exam. Then get pairs to discuss their own opinions of the places and choose three. Elicit the top ones from each pair. Ask the class which other places they would add and why. If necessary, give prompts such as: Mount Everest, China/Nepal; The Great Wall of China; The Pyramids at Giza, Egypt; The Grand Canyon, USA; The Lost City of Machu Picchu, Peru.

> **Answers**
>
> 1 1 Petra   2 Uyuni   3 Masai Mara   4 Forbidden City   5 Uluru
>
> **Suggested answers**
>
> 2 Uyuni – spectacular, like another planet; cold, high up
> Uluru – hot, desolate place; spectacular, mysterious sight
> Petra – ancient rock carvings, amazing skills; hot
> Masai Mara – many kinds of animal, some dangerous; safari; hot
> Forbidden City – ancient, beautiful design, big area to see

Optional activity

Look at the exam task with the class. Make sure that students know what Part 3 consists of. You could ask the following questions. Encourage students to find the answers in the Listening guide on page 95 if they don't already know them.

1 How many people will you hear?
2 Is the information you hear in the same order as the questions?
3 Do the speakers say things that mean the same as A–H?

> **Answers**
>
> 1 five   2 no   3 no – only five of them

3 🔊 1.04 If necessary, explain that the key words are the main 'content' words (as opposed to 'grammatical' words), those that convey the main idea of the sentence. Point out that there are many ways of saying the same (or opposite) thing, but there may be lexical clues, or parallel structures, e.g. *not permitted to / the only way you can* (is something else). Allow a short time for students to underline key words and think of expressions, as these can only be inspired guesses at this stage. Play the recording right through in exam conditions, without pausing.

> **Suggested answers**
>
> B not take, enough water; little/short, etc., should carry, more
> C large animal, attack; tiger/crocodile/lion etc., chase/catch/ escape/eat etc.
> D vehicles, not allowed; car/bus/lorry, etc., mustn't / can / can't / have to
> E expensive, enter; cost/charge/cheap/value, etc., admission/ entry
> F respected, wishes, local people; ignored/agreed/reason, etc., ask/request, inhabitants/live
> G guidebook, carrying, useful; guide, on/with me, useless/ practical
> H All, people, tourists; Everyone/Everybody/Nobody; visitors/ inhabitants/local

Recording script

You will hear five different people talking about going to famous places. For questions 1–5, choose from the list (A–H) what each speaker says about their visit to each site. Use the letters only once. There are three extra letters which you do not need to use.

Speaker 1

Last August in Bolivia we saw the incredible Salar de Uyuni, the world's biggest salt flat, nearly 4,000 metres up in the Andes. We were on a five-day expedition which also took in volcanoes, old mining towns and the astonishing multicoloured lakes there. The views were stunning, and although it was winter and well below freezing at night, the midday sun was really strong. Everything was well organised and good value for money, though <u>bottled water was running a little short by the fourth day. It wasn't easy to find water up there and we should have carried more with us, really.</u> We spent a night in a hotel made entirely of salt and met some of the local people, who were really friendly.

Speaker 2

We approached the Jordanian town of Petra on the Desert Highway, but we had to leave our hire car on the outskirts as <u>the only means of transport you can use there are four-legged: horse, donkey or camel.</u> I suppose we could have walked, but it was hot so we decided to go by camel with a local guide. He spoke excellent English and explained the historical background as we admired the magnificent buildings cut from the rock many centuries ago. It must have been around 40 degrees there and we'd forgotten to take any drinking water with us, but that didn't matter as there were plenty of cafés serving cool drinks along the way.

Speaker 3

When I actually saw Uluru, the huge red rock in central Australia, it took my breath away. Also known as Ayers Rock, it towers 350 metres above the flat surrounding desert, and has religious significance to the native inhabitants who live in and run the Uluru National Park. In fact, when you arrive there and buy an inexpensive two-day pass, <u>they ask you very politely if you would mind not walking on the rock itself, and for that reason we decided to go round it instead.</u> That turned out to be over ten kilometres, rather more than the guidebook said, but we had plenty of water with us. As we left, we saw tourists climbing Uluru, but we were glad we'd chosen not to.

Speaker 4

Visiting the Forbidden City was definitely the highlight of our stay in Beijing. It's a massive place, and <u>I don't know what we would've done without the pocket guide I had with me.</u> You have to pay an admission fee of about six euros, but I thought it was worth it bearing in mind there are nearly a thousand buildings there. We loved the use of the royal colour yellow and I was fascinated by the complex design of everything, but you can't keep walking all day without a break so in the afternoon we stopped at a café that was full of local people. Remarkably, there's now a Starbucks actually inside the Forbidden City!

Speaker 5

We had an absolutely fantastic week in the Masai Mara National Reserve in Kenya. We saw all the big animals you'd expect there: elephants, giraffes, crocodiles and so on, all for just 30 euros a day entry fee. We didn't need to drive, either, because a guide picked us up in a safari vehicle at the hotel each morning. Actually, that's the only way you can get about, because <u>you mustn't go anywhere on foot within the Reserve,</u> presumably because you might meet a hungry lion if you do. And the local guides were great at pointing out animals which on your own you might have missed.

Exam task answers

1 B   2 D   3 F   4 G   5 A

4   Let the class check, then go through the answers, if necessary focusing on the relevant parts of the recording again if any are not clear. If time allows, highlight some of the distraction used in the recording, for example:

Answers

1 good value for money, local people
2 we could have walked, a local guide, we'd forgotten to take any drinking water with us
3 inexpensive, you would mind not walking / we'd chosen not to, guidebook, plenty of water
4 admission fee of about six euros, worth it, local people
5 30 euros a day entry fee, guide

Note: the speakers use a number of modal verb forms, which is the focus of Grammar that follows.

Grammar

Review of modal verbs

1   As well as the focus on modals, there is some useful topic-related vocabulary in this exercise, so be ready to explain terms such as *aircraft*, *platform*, *seat belt*, *accident*, *roadworks*, *traffic jam*, *delayed*, *yacht*. Otherwise, elicit the meanings when you go through the answers. If there is time, ask why the incorrect alternatives are wrong, as in Exercise 2. Encourage students to refer to the Grammar reference on page 104 if necessary.

Answers

1 correct: *could have walked* (past possibility); *could walk* is for past ability
2 correct: *mustn't* (prohibition); *don't have to* is for no obligation
3 correct: *might have* dropped (past possibility); *had to drop* is for past obligation
4 correct: *must* (obligation by the speaker); *have to* is for external obligation
5 correct: *don't have to* (not necessary); *shouldn't* is for something that is the wrong thing to do
6 correct: *may have been* (past possibility); *must have been* is for certainty about the past
7 correct: *needn't have got* (did something unnecessarily); *didn't need to get* is for something not done because it was unnecessary
8 correct: *shouldn't have* (the wrong thing to do in the past); *can't have* is for a past impossibility

2   This activity could be done in pairs. Get students to correct the sentences and decide what kind of mistakes they are, e.g. wrong tense; possibility, not obligation. Go through the answers. If your class tend to make other mistakes with modals, e.g. adding *to* after *must* or *might*, put some of these on the board or OHP and elicit corrections.

Answers

1 *had to buy* (wrong past form of modal verb)
2 *was able to find* (one occasion)
3 *should have been* (it didn't actually happen)
4 *mustn't drive* (not allowed, not unnecessary)
5 *didn't need to call* (wrong past form of modal verb)
6 *don't have to spend* (wrong negative modal verb)
7 *may/might have to stand* (possibility, not ability)
8 *may/might have already heard* (past possibility)

3 Let students use the context to work out for themselves that past forms are needed throughout, but point out that contracted forms such as *must've* are possible here as it is informal dialogue. You may want to practise the pronunciation of these forms, possibly by getting pairs to roleplay the completed dialogue. Check the answers.

> **Answers**
>
> 1 must have missed   2 could have got in   3 might have left
> 4 can't have done   5 had to walk   6 must have switched off
> 7 might even have forgotten   8 must have had

4 Elicit the meaning of the adjective *compulsory* and examples of its use, then get pairs to practise making comments and replying as dialogues. Various answers are possible in most cases, especially negative forms: *You shouldn't have gone to bed so late*, etc. Elicit these when you go through the answers with the class.

> **Suggested answers**
>
> 1 They must be twins.
> 2 You should have gone to bed earlier last night.
> 3 We didn't have to wear a uniform.
> 4 Someone must have stolen it.
> 5 You could have saved some money.
> 6 You shouldn't do that.
> 7 You can't have done!
> 8 You might have spent/lost it.

5 Encourage pairs to speculate using forms such as *it must have got there in a storm, they can't have landed there on purpose, the police might be looking for the pilot*, etc. Elicit some of the most ingenious theories from the class.

Reading and Use of English

Part 5

1 This activity could be done in pairs. Give pairs a minute or two to discuss the points, and then ask the class what they think. If necessary, prompt with questions about which are the least environmentally harmful forms of travelling (usually rail and bus), and which the most (probably air and car).

2 Give students a couple of minutes to look very quickly at the instructions, text and items. Then elicit the answers. Answer any other questions students may have about Reading and Use of English Part 5.

> **Answers**
>
> 1 a single article
> 2 direct questions, incomplete statements, questions on reference words, questions on the meaning of particular words
> 3 three

3 Point out that students will need to read to the end of the text to check all the options, but allow no more than two minutes for them to do so. Then check the answer. Remind them always to start Reading and Use of English Part 5 by gist-reading the whole text, including the title and any introduction.

> **Answer**
>
> The writer's main purpose is: D.

4 Explain that this is an example question and they should ignore the rest of the text and questions 2–6 for now. Give students time to decide on their answer to question 1 and the reasons why the other options are wrong. Then go through all four options. Students then do the exam task on their own. Set a time limit of 15 minutes for this, as they have already read through the text.

> **Answer**
>
> B is correct: the main factors are still the right experience, the right price and convenient departure schedules.
> A Francis wishes this *were* the case, but it isn't.
> C This isn't the *only* thing they are interested in.
> D Francis doesn't mention global warming.

> **Exam task answers**
>
> 1 B   2 A   3 B   4 D   5 B   6 B

5 You may want to give pairs an extra five minutes to compare answers, and decide who's right where they differ. Go through the answers with the class, answering any questions students may have about the language and content of the text.

6 Give pairs plenty of time to find the words and phrases, then go through the answers.

> **Answers**
>
> 1 travelling public   2 departure schedules   3 fly   4 get away
> 5 destination   6 tour operators   7 brochure
> 8 accommodation-only   9 means of transport

7 Encourage pairs to activate vocabulary from Exercise 6 as they discuss the questions. If necessary, prompt with ideas such as hiring a bicycle at your destination, camping, holidaying at home, etc.

Speaking

Adverbs of degree

1 This activity could be done in pairs. The class should be familiar with most of the adverbs in the rules in the Grammar reference on page 105, but they may not appreciate some of the differences in meaning or constraints in their use. These are sometimes tested in Reading and Use of English, particularly Part 1. Answer any vocabulary questions students may have as they study the rules and the dialogue. Don't go through the answers yet.

2 ● 1.05 Play the recording more than once if necessary. Highlight the form *quite a* + adjective as in *quite a long day* (also *rather a* + adjective, which appears in the Speaking Part 3 recording). Point out that answer 5 can only be *really*, but that in most other cases several other adverbs are possible. Elicit other adverbs, including any not actually given here, e.g. *utterly*.

Answers

1 pretty (*also* fairly, quite)
2 slightly (*also* a bit, a little)
3 rather (*also* quite, a bit, a little, extremely, very, really)
4 quite (*also* rather)
5 really
6 a bit (*also* slightly, a little, quite)
7 rather (*also* quite, really)
8 quite (*also* absolutely)
9 totally (*also* quite, absolutely, completely, really)
10 absolutely (*also* quite, completely, really, totally)
11 fairly (*also* pretty, rather, quite)
12 extremely (*also* really, very)

Recording script

Lucas:	So how was the trip to the coast?
Sarah:	It was pretty good, overall. The bus was slightly late, though only ten minutes, and I was rather tired after quite a long day, but once we got out of town I really started to relax.
Lucas:	Yes, sometimes I'm a bit surprised to find that I rather enjoy bus journeys, though the train's much quicker.
Sarah:	Yes, you're quite right, but it was totally impossible to get a cheap ticket.
Lucas:	I know what you mean. I was absolutely astonished to see how much the train costs on a Friday evening. But anyway, it sounds like the bus was fairly comfortable.
Sarah:	Actually, it was extremely comfortable! I slept most of the way.

Part 3

3 Allow a couple of minutes for students to look at the exam task. Go through the answers and answer any other questions they may have about Speaking Part 3.

Answers

1 the other candidate
2 about three minutes
3 a booklet with written prompts: a diagram containing a question plus various options

4 Give students a minute to absorb and discuss the instructions with their partner, then elicit the answers. Point out that in the exam they will both hear the instructions and see the questions with the options.

Answers

Your town wants to attract more tourists.
1 You have to talk to your partner about how the things in the diagram can help bring in more tourists.
2 You have to decide which two things would attract most visitors to the town.

5 *1.06* Play the recording once, without pausing. Then elicit the answers, reminding the class of the importance of taking turns and talking about every prompt. Point out that they don't actually have to agree with their partner's final choice, but that they should be polite if they do disagree.

Answers

1 yes
2 yes
3 They both choose the carnival, but whereas Laura's second choice is the art gallery, Jonas's is the boat rides.

Recording script

Teacher:	Now, I'd like you to talk about something together for about two minutes. I'd like you to imagine that your town wants to attract more tourists. Here are some things that may help make a town more attractive to visitors. Talk to each other about how these things could help bring in more tourists. You now have some time to look at the task. *[15-second pause]* Could you start now, please?
Jonas:	Right, shall I start?
Laura:	Yes, go ahead.
Jonas:	Well, first there's the theatre. I think that could be quite a good one, because it would attract some fairly rich people, and they would spend more in the town.
Laura:	Yes, but there's only one theatre. Don't you think we'd need lots of them to make much difference to the number of visitors to the town?
Jonas:	That's true.
Laura:	So how about the next one – the carnival? Think of all the people who go to the one in Rio. Maybe we'd get crowds like that here. Or a bit like them, anyway.
Jonas:	Er, well, at least the weather here is fairly good in summer, almost like Brazil. And it'd be really good fun to set up, too.
Laura:	Talking about summer, we could have the boat rides, too. So people can cool off a bit in all that tropical heat. That would look pretty good in the town's brochure: smiling couples in rowing boats, picnics next to the lake. Stuff like that.
Jonas:	Yes, maybe. And what about including the bus tour? That's open-air, too.
Laura:	I'm not sure. It's only a small town, so it'd be rather a short tour. Or else they'd have to keep going round and round it. Either way, it might not be very popular with visitors.
Jonas:	The marathon might be better. There's some absolutely stunning countryside round here, and we could get some great photos of people running through it.
Laura:	Yes, I agree. Though from what I've seen of marathons in other cities and countries, it tends to be the local people who come out to watch them, rather than tourists.
Jonas:	Hmm, you may be right. OK, that's five of them done. Let's look at the last one, the art gallery.
Laura:	I quite like that one. It'd show the cultural side of the town, and there are some pretty good local artists.
Jonas:	Yes, and some of them have painted landscapes of the countryside we were talking about just now.
Laura:	Right.
Teacher:	Thank you. Now you have a minute to decide which two things would attract most visitors to the town.

Laura:	OK, I'll start this time if you like.
Jonas:	Fine.
Laura:	Which two shall we choose? I'd go for the art gallery and the carnival. I think that'd make a lot of people want to come to the town. And you?
Jonas:	Definitely the carnival. But instead of the art gallery, I'd choose the boat rides. They would be much more popular, I think.
Laura:	OK, so we agree on one but not the other. That's fine.
Jonas:	I agree.
Teacher:	Thank you.

6 ◯ *1.06* If necessary, explain the meaning of *speculate* and give examples using past modals, e.g. *It might have been … but I'm not sure*. When students have finished, play the recording again – and if necessary for a third time. Then check that everyone has the right answers, as they will be using these expressions when they do the exam task themselves.

> **Answers**
>
> 1 shall I   2 that could be   3 how about   4 we could
> 5 what about   6 it might not be   7 Let's look at   8 I'd go for

7 Make sure students change partners. Explain that this may make the task more similar to the actual exam, where they could be with someone they don't know. Time the activity, stopping after exactly two minutes. Ask the class whether they had time to talk about all the things, and which two most of them chose.

8 Give pairs a minute to talk about whether they feel they took turns properly and both had about the same speaking time. When they've finished, ask the class how any imbalances can be rectified, such as by suggesting that each candidate has a similar number of turns as those on the recording.

Reading and Use of English

Dependent prepositions

1 Point out that Part 1 often tests words and phrases followed by prepositions. Explain that dependent prepositions are a kind of collocation, as many of these adjectives and phrases cannot be used in the same way and with the same meaning without the preposition. Look at the examples with the class. Encourage students to think about each given word in turn, deciding which preposition 'sounds' right and writing the word with the correct preposition. Then, in pairs, they add perhaps three more of their own words with each preposition. Go through the answers, giving and/or eliciting examples. Take particular care with idiomatic phrases such as *about to* and *no sign of*, and also any potential false cognates, e.g. *prepared*, *sensitive*, *regard*. Also get everyone to note down the correct additions suggested by the class. Finally, point out that some of the phrases they have completed tend to be used mainly in formal letters (see Unit 5 Writing).

> **Answers**
>
> | | |
> |---|---|
> | word/phrase + *to*: | in relation, in response, obliged, prepared, required, sensitive, supposed, with regard (*also* about, belong, bound, compared, object, opposed, tend, thanks) |
> | word/phrase + *with*: | familiar, fed up, in connection, involved, (have) nothing to do, obsessed, the trouble (*also* agree, along, associated, beginning, compared, disappointed, have a word, pleased, satisfied) |
> | word/phrase + *of*: | ashamed, capable, conscious, in need, in place, in terms, in view, informed, sort (*also* afraid, approve, aware, jealous, no sign, proud, take care) |

2 Point out that some of the missing prepositions are *of*, *to* and *with*, but others are not. When students working on their own or in pairs have chosen the correct prepositions, go through each one, eliciting more examples. Point out that in some cases other prepositions are possible, e.g. *compared with*, *responsible to*, and give examples.

> **Answers**
>
> 1 D   2 C   3 A   4 D   5 B   6 A

Part 1

3 Give students a few minutes to study the task – it may take them a little while to be able to answer the third question. Go through the answers and answer any other questions students may have about Use of English Part 1.

> **Answers**
>
> 1 eight
> 2 four
> 3 All four are the same kind of word with some kind of link in meaning.

4 Give the class only a minute to decide what the text is about, then elicit the answer. Once the topic has been established, move on to the exam task.

> **Suggested answers**
>
> what happens in the Barranquilla Carnival, Colombia
> *or*
> what makes Colombia's Barranquilla Carnival so good

Allow students – working on their own – to spend about 15 minutes on the exam task, although they will have slightly less time in the actual exam.

> **Exam task answers**
>
> 1 D   2 A   3 C   4 B   5 D   6 A   7 A   8 B

5 Give students a couple of minutes to check, then elicit the answers. Many of the options are B2-level vocabulary items which you may want to focus on as you go through the answers.

6 If you have students from different countries or regions, get them to tell each other about a carnival or a similar event they may not be familiar with. Encourage the use

of expressions containing dependent prepositions and language from the text and options. Also suggest that they use expressions for comparing from Unit 2 Speaking.

Writing

Part 1 essay

1 Explain that these are known as addition links and point out that they – and most expressions like them – usually begin a paragraph, sentence or clause, and are followed by a comma. Elicit the answers and tell the class to use them to introduce main points in their essays and other writing such as formal letters.

> **Answers**
> a First of all, For one thing, In the first place
> b For another thing, Next
> c Lastly
> d On balance, To conclude

2 This activity could be done in pairs. Allow a minute for discussion of the instructions and the questions. Then go through the answers, suggesting that students ask themselves questions like these every time they do a Writing Part 1 task.

> **Answers**
> 1 you have had a discussion in an English class and you have been asked to write an essay; the advantages and disadvantages of taking holidays near home rather than travelling abroad
> 2 your teacher
> 3 whether it is better to have holidays near home rather than travel abroad
> 4 which is cheaper, which is better for the environment, and your own idea
> 5 reasons for your point of view

3 Pairs do the gist-reading for the answers to questions 1 and 2 quickly, then scan for the addition links. Check their answers and elicit more addition links.

> **Answers**
> 1 holidays abroad
> 2 2nd: cheaper, 3rd: better for the environment, 4th: own idea
> 3 to begin with, secondly, finally, to sum up
> 4 first of all, next, then, lastly, in conclusion, to conclude, on balance, etc.

4 Give pairs a few minutes to scan the text. Then elicit the answers.

> **Answers**
> 1 should not 2 however 3 locations
> 4 inexpensive (also: budget, economical) 5 can be done
> 6 cannot 6 I am absolutely convinced (that)

5 Allow 35 minutes for the actual writing. Students will have 40 minutes in the exam, but that includes time for studying the input material and planning their work – which they have already done – and for checking, which is the focus of the next exercise.

6 Give students a couple of minutes to check their work. If you prefer peer correction, give pairs five minutes to make suggestions about each other's work, and for them to make any changes.

Model answer

These days many people are choosing not to travel abroad for their holidays. There are several reasons for this.

The main reason is financial. In the current economic climate, people have less money for their leisure pursuits. Holidays abroad are not cheap. Additional expenses include the purchase of a visa for some countries, and the need to buy travel insurance and foreign currency.

Another important reason for holidaying at home is the effect foreign travel has on the environment. Air travel produces more pollution than any other form of transport, so is the least green.

People also feel safer in their own country. They are used to the food and water, so they feel they are less likely to become ill. And, if necessary, they can more easily return home.

This year I have decided to stay at home. In fact, I'm going to sleep in my own bed every night. There are many beautiful places in my country which foreign visitors come to see. I want to enjoy these places too. And some of them, I can visit by bike!

Revision

1 **Answers**
> 2 mustn't hit 3 must have ridden *or* must have been riding
> 4 shouldn't have spent 5 can't have seen
> 6 mightn't / might not have taken 7 needn't have cooked

2 Point out that more than one answer may be possible.

> **Answers**
> 2 have to check in (*or* need to)
> 3 must've / must have gone home early
> 4 didn't need to go to college
> 5 had to wear life jackets
> 6 should've / should have put petrol in the car
> 7 might've / might have had the wrong address (*or* may've / may have *or* could've / could have)

3 **Answers**
> 1 D 2 A 3 B 4 B 5 C 6 C

4 **Answers**
> 1 with 2 of 3 of 4 with 5 at 6 of 7 to 8 of 9 with
> 10 of

> Remind students that there is more practice on the CD-ROM.

4 Taking time out

Unit objectives

TOPICS	entertainment (film, music, arts), leisure
GRAMMAR	verbs followed by *to* + infinitive or *-ing*, *too* and *enough*, review of present perfect
VOCABULARY	phrasal verbs with *on*
READING and	Part 6: focusing on an item, writer's attitude
USE OF ENGLISH	Part 4: present perfect
WRITING	Part 2 review: descriptive adjectives, recommendations
LISTENING	Part 4: focusing on key words in items
SPEAKING	Part 4: asking for and justifying opinions, giving reasons and examples

Reading and Use of English

Part 6

1 This activity could be done in pairs. Allow students to use dictionaries for this. Be ready to help out where necessary with pronunciation, especially that of *audience*, *gig*, *lyrics*, *scene* and *venue*. Also point out that *gig* is quite informal.

2 Point out that question 1 is a similar activity to that in Speaking Part 2. For question 2, prompt if necessary with suggestions such as *applaud* (theatre), *dance* (pop concert), *get an icecream* (cinema), *talk* (art gallery); then *use a mobile phone* (theatre), *record the entire performance* (pop concert), *talk* (cinema), *touch the exhibits* (art gallery). You may want to mention that question 2 introduces the topic of the text.

3 Remind the class to skim right through the text to get the gist. Reading just the opening, for instance, might give the impression the answer is C.

> **Answer**
> B

4 These questions remind students of some of the kinds of link they need to look for in this task type. Give them no more than two minutes to answer the questions, then elicit the answers to these questions only. Allow no more than 20 minutes for students working on their own to do the exam task, in exam conditions.

> **Answers**
> 1 D (reaction)
> 2 this
> 3 After saying the reaction was understandable, the writer supports this by saying *Who hasn't been to ...* , claiming that everyone has had a similar experience.

> **Exam task answers**
> 1 D 2 B 3 A 4 F 5 G 6 C

5 When students have finished checking their work, go through the answers, answering any language questions they may have apart from any relating to phrasal verbs with *on*.

Phrasal verbs with *on*

6 Get students to work out the meanings of the phrasal verbs, then go through the answers with the class.

> **Answers**
> 1 depends on   2 continued   3 stand on   4 continued

7 Point out that in some cases students will need to use the past form of the verb, but none of these sentences requires the addition of any words apart from the base verb and *on*. Go through the answers, eliciting the meaning of *critics* in sentence 4.

> **Answers**
> 2 log on   3 carried on   4 depends on   5 sit on   6 played on
> 7 turn on   8 based on   9 count on   10 focuses on

Listening

Part 4

1 Students could discuss these questions as a class or in pairs. Mention YouTube or similar websites as likely sources, and suggest music and personal videos as possible favourites.

2 **1.07** You may want to refer students back to Listening in Unit 1 for an example script with a focus on distractors in multiple-choice questions. Then, returning to this page, get the class to study the Quick steps and say what the exam instructions tell them they are going to hear. Focus attention on just the question in item 1, pointing out that the key words have been underlined. Play the recording of the first exchange between the Interviewer and Sonia, twice if necessary. Elicit the answers.

> **Suggested answers**
> 1 most want – main interest, girl – child
> 2 B – *colour paintings* were her *main interest then*
> 3 A – she *worked on sculptures*, but later, *when I grew up* and was *at art college*
> C – referring to drawing in the interviewer's question, she says *I tended to see it as just the first step in creating colour paintings*

> **Recording script**
>
> *You will hear part of a radio interview with Sonia Evans, an artist whose work first became popular on the Internet. For questions 1–7, choose the best answer (A, B or C).*
>
> Interviewer: My guest today is artist Sonia Evans, whose drawings have become popular on the Internet and elsewhere. Tell me, Sonia, have you always been keen on drawing?

> Sonia: Yes, but as a child I tended to see it as just the first step in creating colour paintings, which were my main interest then. When I grew up I realised I didn't really have an eye for colour, and although at art college I worked on sculptures for a while I eventually went back to doing pictures, though this time just with a pencil. And that's what I've been doing ever since.

3 `1.08` Students do the underlining quickly. When they have finished, ask the class which words they have underlined, bearing in mind that these are bound to be quite subjective choices. Then play the whole recording through without pausing.

Suggested answers

2 disappointed, exhibition   3 decided, Internet, because
4 Sonia's video, different   5 feel, how many, looked
6 result, success   7 react, negative comments

Recording script

You will hear part of a radio interview with Sonia Evans, an artist whose work first became popular on the Internet. For questions 1–7, choose the best answer (A, B or C).

Interviewer: My guest today is artist Sonia Evans, whose drawings have become popular on the Internet and elsewhere. Tell me, Sonia, have you always been keen on drawing?

Sonia: Yes, but as a child I tended to see it as just the first step in creating (1) <u>colour paintings, which were my main interest then</u>. When I grew up I realised I didn't really have an eye for colour, and although at art college I worked on sculptures for a while I eventually went back to doing pictures, though this time just with a pencil. And that's what I've been doing ever since.

Interviewer: So when did you first display any of your work?

Sonia: Quite some time ago, at the art gallery in my home town. I was really excited when they agreed to show some of my drawings, though that feeling didn't last when I realised the so-called exhibition was taking place in a tiny place outside the main building. Of course, it was never my aim to sell any of them, but (2) <u>it would have been nice if more than a handful of visitors to the gallery had actually realised they were there</u>. The fact that the art critic in the local paper was quite impressed didn't help much, as he didn't write about them until the day after the exhibition had ended.

Interviewer: That must have been quite annoying.

Sonia: Yes, it was. I didn't bother trying to have anything else shown there after that.

Interviewer: And what made you decide to put your work online?

Sonia: A photographer friend of mine had the idea first, though he never actually got round to doing it. And (3) <u>as the only alternative was to move to a big city and try to get noticed there, something that didn't appeal to me at all, I felt that going online was the best thing to do</u>.

Interviewer: And how did you actually go about it?

Sonia: I made a short video of myself drawing. Of course, there were already lots like that on YouTube – there were too many to count, in fact – but (4) <u>mine was unique at the time in that I left the drawing unfinished</u>. So although others were often by people who could handle a video camera better than me, and probably had just as much artistic ability too, it was mine that made viewers want to come back three days later to find out what the subject actually was.

Interviewer: And that created a lot of interest, did it?

Sonia: Well, yes, probably because I'm quite good at disguising what I'm drawing. Anyway, an astonishing number of people viewed the second video. There were literally tens of thousands of hits from all over the world. And the strange thing was that I should have been delighted by figures like those, or at least relieved that at last my work was out there, but instead (5) <u>I had the uneasy sensation that there were too many hits</u>.

Interviewer: How long did that feeling last?

Sonia: I got over it quickly enough once I'd done a few more videos. In fact, I started going to the opposite extreme.

Interviewer: How do you mean?

Sonia: When I realised how well they were doing, I started to become a bit too obsessed with the number of hits they were getting – logging on to check them dozens of times a day, and getting really stressed whenever they slowed down a little. I found myself (6) <u>staying up later and later</u> to keep an eye on them, because of course many of the hits were from different time zones, <u>and getting up earlier and earlier the next day</u>. So then I'd find it hard to stay awake in the daytime, to the point where I didn't have enough time to do my work properly.

Interviewer: Not so good.

Sonia: No, and it got even worse when I started reading reviews of my videos on those websites that specialise in criticising online videos.

Interviewer: They were bad, were they?

Sonia: Some of them, yes. There were attacks on the quality of my work, and some quite personal stuff, too.

Interviewer: What was your reaction?

Sonia: Well, fortunately I'm not someone who suffers from depression or anything like that, but (7) <u>I decided to keep well away from those sites</u>. They just made me feel angry and want to write back to the people who wrote those things, but of course I didn't. And nowadays I never even think about them. Especially since my work started to appear in other media.

Interviewer: Yes, I'm sure quite a few of our listeners will recognise your name from magazines, and now from radio, too. Thank you, Sonia.

Sonia: Thank you.

Exam task answers

2 A   3 A   4 C   5 A   6 B   7 C

4 When everyone has made sure they have answered all the questions, check the answers.

Grammar

Verbs followed by *to* + infinitive or *-ing*

1 This activity could be done in pairs. Focus on the example (sentence a), and also, if necessary, on the *-ing* form in sentence c. Give students a minute to note down their answers, then check. Point out that *get round to* is followed by *-ing* (like *look forward to*), as *to* is part of the phrasal verb. Elicit more verbs that can be followed by either *to* or *-ing* without any change in meaning, e.g. *begin, continue.*

> **Answers**
> 1 *to* + infinitive: b agree, f start
>   *-ing*: c (not) bother, d get round to, e start
> 2 *start* with no change in meaning

2 Ask pairs to think of an example sentence for each verb, then decide which form follows the verb. Go through their examples when they have finished. Then elicit more verbs in each category, and get the class to note these down, too. If necessary, ask about specific common verbs, e.g. *hope, plan, practise.*

> **Answers**
> *to* + infinitive: appear, expect, learn, manage, offer, promise, refuse, seem, threaten, want
> *-ing*: avoid, dislike, enjoy, finish, imagine, insist on, keep (on), mind, miss, suggest

3 Get pairs to match these sentence halves and discuss the differences in meaning, then go through these with the class. Elicit more examples with each pair of verb forms, using different verb tenses and situations.

> **Answers**
> 1 a-ii (continued the same activity), b-i (changed activity)
> 2 a-ii (as an experiment), b-i (it was impossible)
> 3 a-ii (you're sorry about a past action), b-i (you're sorry about what you're going to have to say)
> 4 a-i (something that stays in your memory for a long time), b-ii (something you should do)
> 5 a-ii (you haven't wanted to speak to them since then), b-i (you were walking but you stood still and spoke to them)
> 6 a-i (remember something from the past), b-ii (remember to do something in the future)

4 To make this exercise a little easier for weaker classes, tell them that all the mistakes require changing *-ing* forms to *to* + infinitive, or vice versa. Give students working on their own or in pairs a minute or so to do this, then go through the answers, eliciting more examples using the target verbs.

> **Answers**
> 1 agreed to help 2 suggested buying 3 forgot to ask
> 4 remember being 5 mind working 6 go on behaving

5 Students can complete the news story individually or in pairs. Help out with any new language, such as *downturn.* Go through the answers with the class.

> **Answers**
> 1 to show 2 to indicate 3 going 4 to spend 5 to see
> 6 rising

6 Give pairs two minutes to discuss the questions, using the target structures. Encourage the use of more verbs with *to* + infinitive and *-ing*, such as *want to see, avoid watching, seem to be.*

7 You may want the class to work in different pairs to avoid any repetition from the previous exercise. Point out that they don't have to use every verb in the three exercises, but where they do they must be careful with the form of the second verb (*-ing* or *to*). Monitor for accuracy.

Speaking

too and *enough*

1 Explain to the class that as well as presenting and practising forms that will be useful in Speaking, this section continues the focus on *to* + infinitive and *-ing* forms. Point out that *too* is often confused with *very*, and that incorrect positioning of *enough* is another common mistake – as students will see in Exercise 2. Give pairs time to study and discuss the examples and questions, then elicit the rules from the class, with more examples in each case.

> **Answers**
> a too b too c enough d too e enough
> 1 before, no 2 after, before 3 *to* + infinitive

2 Students working on their own or in pairs correct these very typical mistakes, preferably by writing out the complete sentences to reinforce the right forms. Go through the answers with the class, if necessary referring them back to the rules in Exercise 1.

> **Answers**
> 1 too lazy 2 too many people 3 enough leisure time
> 4 early enough 5 The streets here are too narrow
> 6 very bad news

3 Point out that *too/enough … for* are useful structures for Speaking and Writing, and are also sometimes tested in Reading and Use of English, especially Part 4. Go through the examples, stressing the importance of not repeating the object after the final infinitive if there is one in the original sentence (not *the DVD was too expensive for me to buy it*). Allow plenty of time for the class to write two sentences for each item, prompting if necessary with a suitable adjective to go with *enough* as the main focus of this exercise is the overall structure, not antonyms.

> **Answers**
> 2 This computer is too slow for me to watch films on.
>   This computer isn't fast/quick/powerful enough for me to watch films on.
> 3 It was too noisy for us to hear what was going on.
>   It wasn't quiet enough for us to hear what was going on.
> 4 That book was too long for me to read in a week.
>   That book wasn't short enough for me to read in a week.
> 5 That bed was too uncomfortable for me to sleep on.
>   That bed wasn't comfortable enough for me to sleep on.

Part 4

4 Students could do the matching activity in pairs. The expressions themselves should not present any difficulties, but remind them to use a polite tone when asking the questions, especially *Why do you think so?*, etc. Go through the answers, modelling this.

> ### Answers
>
> 1 *Asking for opinions:* What's your opinion?, What do you think?, What are your feelings about this?, How do you feel about ... ?
> 2 *Asking for reasons:* Why do you think so?, Is that because ... ?, Could you tell me why?, Any particular reason?
> 3 *Giving reasons:* because ... , for one thing ... , so ... , The main reason is that ...
> 4 *Giving examples:* for example ... , for instance ... , like ... , such as ...

5 🔘 *1.09* Tell the class to look at the questions before they listen and explain that in the actual exam they speak to the 'interlocutor'. You may want to point out that the examiners will have a list of questions to choose from in the exam, and are unlikely to use all the available questions. Then play the recording once, as students focus on the teacher to answer the first question in the instructions, and the two candidates for the second and third.

> ### Answers
>
> The teacher asks questions 1, 4 and 6. Daniela does this part of the Speaking text better – because she gives fuller answers, responding to what Julian says in her comments, giving reasons and examples. She also asks her partner for his opinions, and the reason for them.

Recording script

Teacher: Julian, what are the advantages and disadvantages of having lots of leisure time?

Julian: Er, you can do many things, like go to the cinema, or look at things on the Internet. And the disadvantages are that you can get quite bored if there isn't much to do, and maybe spend too much time watching TV.

Daniela: Yes, you can waste your time, especially if you don't plan your free time well. But everyone needs to have leisure time because often they do too much work and it's not good only to work or study all the time. You can use it to learn to do new things, too.

Teacher: Which hobby or interest would you most like to take up, Daniela?

Daniela: Dancing, I think. Probably salsa dancing. The main reason is that it's pretty simple to learn, and it's lots and lots of fun. The music is fantastic too. I've always liked it, particularly the salsa music from Colombia.

Teacher: And which hobby or interest would you most like to take up, Julian?

Julian: I'd like to have a big dog and take it out for long walks in the country. I've wanted to have a dog for a while. But I can't keep one at home. *[short pause]*

Daniela: Could you tell me why?

Julian: Well, we've just moved to a smaller flat and although I haven't asked my parents yet, I think they'll say there isn't enough room, that it wouldn't be fair to keep a big dog there. I suppose I'll have to wait until I get my own house.

Teacher: Daniela, do you think people these days read fewer books than previous generations did?

Daniela: I'm not sure. In the past in my country not many people read books, but all that has changed now. There are more novels specially for young people, about modern society, so more people buy them, I think. Also it is very easy to find any book you like on the Internet, in online bookshops or auction sites, and they will send it to you quickly by post. If you have a credit card, of course! So no, I don't believe that people read less now. What do you think?

Julian: Well I don't think people read less these days, but maybe not so many books. I mean, there are so many magazines and newspapers and articles that you can read on the Internet. There's isn't enough time to read books too.

Daniela: Maybe people read books at different times. For instance, on the Metro, or on the beach. You can't really take your computer there with you. Also, some people say that reading from a screen all the time is very bad for your eyes, that a book is much better. What's your opinion?

Julian: Actually, that may be true. I know my eyes have been getting sore since I began reading a lot of texts online last year. I've already had to start using reading glasses.

Teacher: Thank you, that's the end of the test.

6 🔘 *1.09* Playing the recording once more should be sufficient, as only one candidate (Daniela) uses the expressions in Exercise 4 and there is quite a lot of text between each expression. Check the answers, and highlight the polite intonation of the questions again.

> ### Answers
>
> because ... , The main reason is that ... , Could you tell me why?, so ... , What do you think?, for instance ... , What's your opinion?

7 In order to make this activity more similar to the exam situation, you may want to put students into groups that do not include their usual partners. Tell the 'examiners' to ask the same three or four questions to each 'candidate', unless the candidates themselves ask each other to comment – which should be encouraged. Give everyone a minute to look at the questions, then time the groups so that they speak for no more than four minutes. Encourage them to use some of the suggested language, but point out that neither candidates nor examiners should be so concerned with grammatical accuracy that fluency suffers.

8 Remind the examiners to be constructive and diplomatic in their comments. Ask the class whether they encountered any practical difficulties, and if so deal with these before they next do this activity in Unit 8.

Reading and Use of English

Review of present perfect

1 This activity could be done in pairs. Give students a few minutes to do the task, then check everyone has the correct answers. Point out that the present perfect continuous tense emphasises the length of a recent or continuing event, but we cannot use it with stative verbs like *believe* or *want*. Elicit the negative and interrogative forms of both present perfect tenses, and some example sentences, including sentences with *for* and *since*. Then give some examples with *already*, *yet* and *just*, and elicit more sentences.

> **Answers**
>
> 1 a past simple, b present perfect continuous, c present perfect
> 2 a already, b for, c yet, d since, e just

2 Go through the answers once students, working on their own or in pairs, have finished correcting the mistakes.

> **Answers**
>
> 1 I've been living   2 what I did last month   3 for a month *or* since a month ago   4 I've / I have already printed   5 We've been waiting   6 hasn't ended yet

Part 4

3 Focus attention on both sentences and the word in capitals in the example. Elicit the answers to questions 1–4, pointing out that students should look for the changes in grammar and vocabulary that need to be made whenever they do Key Word Transformations. Explain that a mark is given for each element of the correct answer, so if they don't know the whole answer they should write as much of it as they can.

> **Answers**
>
> 1 for
> 2 past simple to present perfect (negative)
> 3 *last* is not used
> 4 haven't / have not been there = 1 mark, for = 1 mark

4 Students do the exam task individually, writing down the changes they make as in Exercise 3.

> **Exam task answers**
>
> 1 light enough | (for me) to (*because + so → enough + for*)
> 2 carried on | reading (*verb + infinitive → phrasal verb + -ing*)
> 3 haven't done ballet | since (*verb + -ing → negative present perfect + since*)
> 4 too complicated | for any of (*so ... that + none → too ... for + any*)
> 5 've/have been learning Chinese | for (*present perfect + since → present perfect continuous + for*)
> 6 count on | winning (*will + infinitive → phrasal verb + -ing*)

5 Give the class a minute to check for accuracy. As you go through the answers, elicit these changes in each case. Point out that students may well see similar patterns in practice tests – and in the exam itself.

Writing

Part 2 review

1 Students look quickly at the exam task and questions. Elicit the answers and remind students to ask themselves similar questions whenever they do this kind of task.

> **Answers**
>
> 1 international readers of an English-language magazine
> 2 information on the setting, story and main characters, and your recommendation to other readers on whether they should read the novel or not
> 3 between 140 and 190

2 This activity could be done in pairs. Give students plenty of time to answer the questions, and answer any questions students may have about any language apart from the words in question 3. Go through the answers, then ask the class whether they think they would enjoy a book like this, and if so, why.

> **Answers**
>
> 1 paragraph 1: c, paragraph 2: d, paragraph 3: b, paragraph 4: a
> 2 quite formal: no contracted forms; some long, less common words; formal structures (e.g. *in which*); complex sentences (e.g. second sentence of third paragraph)
> 3 a plot, b fast-paced, c gripping, d convincing, e impressive, f themes, g tense
> 4 Yes. *If you enjoy a tense thriller which is quick and easy to read, I suggest you choose this one.*

3 Get students to use their dictionaries for any new words, or – if time is short – elicit the meanings with one example each. Also focus on some useful antonyms, such as *unpredictable*, *unremarkable* and *fast-moving*. Make sure that students have identified the six negative words, though opinions may differ about some, e.g., *absurd*, *bizarre*. Finally, ask the class if they know any other useful descriptive adjectives.

> **Suggested answers**
>
> dreadful, poor, predictable, slow-moving

4 Point out that these expressions can be used to review films, CDs, holidays, etc., as well as books. If students have difficulty with the use of any of the expressions, prompt by filling in some of the gaps, e.g. *My advice is to avoid this novel and instead read something by (name of author).*

> **Answers**
>
> *To recommend something:*
> This ... is really worth ... because ...
> This is one of the best ... I have ever ... , so I suggest ...
> Anyone who likes ... will really enjoy this ...
> *To say not to do something:*
> My advice is to avoid this ... and instead ...
> I would advise everyone to ... a better ... than this, such as ...

5 Allow a maximum of 35–40 minutes for writing as students have already studied the task, reminding them to leave

at least five minutes to check their work. Alternatively, students could write a draft, possibly as homework, then work in pairs to compare and improve what they have written. They might then do the peer correction in Exercise 6 with a different partner.

6 This checking task could be done as a peer correction activity. As a follow-up activity at a later date, the class could be asked to write a review of a film, play or TV programme.

Model answer

The Strange Case of Dr Jekyll and Mr Hyde

The famous novel *The Strange Case of Dr Jekyll and Mr Hyde* was written in the late nineteenth century by the Scottish author Robert Louis Stevenson. It is set in the foggy London of the time, which helps to give many of the scenes a mysterious atmosphere.

The story is told by Gabriel Utterson, a lawyer friend of Henry Jekyll, a wealthy doctor who has an interest in unusual scientific experiments. Jekyll's behaviour becomes increasingly weird as the plot develops. The other main character is Edward Hyde, an ugly, violent man whose repulsive appearance and manner make people react with horror and fear.

When Hyde commits a series of brutal crimes, Utterson and Hastie Lanyon, another close friend of Jekyll, become concerned about the apparent links between Hyde and the doctor. Eventually, following Hyde's death, Utterson discovers that Dr Jekyll had in fact drunk a liquid that totally changed his personality, turning him into the absolutely evil Mr Hyde.

Even though it was written so long ago, this is one of the best science-fiction novels I have ever read. I would strongly recommend reading it.

Revision

1 | **Answers**

1 regret not | going
2 has been doing gymnastics *or* has been a gymnast | since
3 insisted on | paying for *or* insisted (that) he | paid for
4 keeps on | breaking
5 too difficult for | all pianists *or* any pianists
6 hasn't sung here | for

2 | **Answers**

1 How long have you been learning English? I've / I have been learning English for X years.
2 How many times have you been to the theatre? I've / I have been to the theatre X times. *or* I've / I have never been to the theatre.
3 Have you had your evening meal yet? Yes, I've / I have had my evening meal (already). *or* No, I haven't / have not had my evening meal yet.
4 Have you been listening to the radio for the last hour? Yes, I've / I have been listening to the radio for the last hour. *or* No, I haven't / have not been listening to the radio for the last hour.
5 Have you just spoken to your partner? Yes, I've / I have just spoken to him/her. *or* No, I haven't / I have not just spoken to him/her.

3 This exercise could be done in pairs with students also asking each other follow-up questions using the target language.

| **Answers**

1 listening   2 to do   3 to do   4 having to   5 to do   6 to play
7 hearing   8 not doing

4 | **Answers**

Across
1 scene   2 live   4 work   5 fine   7 superb   8 theme   10 plot
12 shot   13 critic   14 lyrics   15 gig
Down
1 script   3 venue   6 gripping   7 set   9 moving   11 poor
12 solo   13 cast

Remind students that there is more practice on the CD-ROM.

5 Learning and earning

Unit objectives

TOPICS	education, study and learning, careers and jobs
GRAMMAR	review of future forms, countable and uncountable nouns
VOCABULARY	phrasal verbs with *take*; noun suffixes: -or, -ist, -ian, -er, -ant
READING and USE OF ENGLISH	Part 7: focusing on key words Part 3: suffixes, countable and uncountable nouns
WRITING	Part 2 letter of application: formal expressions, achieving aims
LISTENING	Part 2: predicting text content
SPEAKING	Part 1: talking about future plans

Listening

Part 2

1 Focus attention on the photos, allow a minute's discussion in pairs or small groups, then elicit the answers with reasons. Ask if anyone knows which universities they are. Make sure that everyone knows where New Zealand is. You may wish to mention that Harvard is in fact in Cambridge, i.e. Cambridge, Massachusetts.

> **Answers**
>
> 1 USA (Harvard)   2 New Zealand (Canterbury at Christchurch)
> 3 UK (Cambridge)   4 Australia (John Curtin School of Medical Research, Canberra)

2 ● 1.10 This text-completion task could be done in pairs, with the help of dictionaries if necessary. For some classes, most of these words will be cognates in their first language. Play the recording so that students can check their answers, then go through the answers and make sure that the meaning of each word is fully understood.

> **Recording script**
>
> The higher education systems in some English-speaking countries such as the UK, Australia and New Zealand are similar in some ways. Pupils at secondary school take examinations at the age of 18, and those who qualify for university then usually begin their Bachelor's degree courses, which normally last three or four years. At this stage students are known as undergraduates, and they learn about their subject by attending lectures in large groups. These are often followed by discussion in seminars, involving a much smaller group of students and a tutor who asks questions and encourages them to talk about the topic. When they successfully finish their first degree, students graduate and may then go on to do a postgraduate course such as a Master's degree. For most students, the highest academic achievement is to obtain a doctoral degree by writing a thesis based on research.

> **Answers**
>
> 1 secondary   2 qualify   3 Bachelor's   4 undergraduates
> 5 lectures   6 seminars   7 tutor   8 graduate
> 9 postgraduate   10 Master's   11 academic   12 thesis

Optional activity

Ask the class the following questions (or put students into small groups to discuss them): *What do you know about New Zealand? What is the country famous for?* Get students to talk about its location, geography, climate, people and language, e.g. its indigenous Maori people, sport (especially rugby and mountaineering), food exports, kiwi bird (and fruit), setting for *Lord of the Rings*. Point out that New Zealand has spectacular scenery but a relatively small population, and that Christchurch is the biggest city in the South Island, with just 300,000 inhabitants. The class may recall hearing about the earthquake there of February 2011.

3 Give pairs two or three minutes to discuss the questions, then quickly elicit some answers.

> **Answers**
>
> 1 A student talks about going from Europe to university in New Zealand.
> 2 Suggested answers: to go to a good university, to do a particular course, to experience a new culture, to improve her English, to meet new people, to become more independent, to be near the sea and mountains, etc.
> 3 Suggested answers: advantages – different academic system, different country, new challenges, travel, make new friends; disadvantages – distance from home country, time difference, adapting to new culture, having to make new friends, possible language difficulties, different food

4 ● 1.11 Give pairs a few minutes to look at all the questions, possibly referring back to a similar activity on page 18 in Unit 2 (Exercise 2). Elicit the answers from the class, bearing in mind there may be more than one possibility in many cases.

> **Suggested answers**
>
> 1 person   2 sport or hobby   3 noun (phrase)   4 noun (phrase)
> 5 noun (phrase)   6 verb (+ noun)   7 verb   8 place or noun
> 9 date   10 noun (phrase)

Go through the Quick steps, then get students to work on their own. Play the recording through twice without pausing.

> **Recording script**
>
> *You will hear European student Alba Ortega talking about going to university in New Zealand. For questions 1–10, complete the sentences.*
>
> *Alba*
>
> What made me want to come to New Zealand? Well, my teacher at school told me about the high academic standards here, and one of my friends had already decided to study in Perth, Australia. But (1) the person who influenced me most was my cousin, who did her first degree here and loved every minute of it. She was in Wellington, but often came down to the South Island for the scenery and sports.

That was something that attracted me to Christchurch in particular, though whereas she came for the winter sports (2) it was the opportunities for rock climbing that really appealed to me. Although now I've actually seen those fantastic mountains I think I'll give skiing a try sometime.

As for the university itself, I mentioned the academic standards as something that's important to me, and (3) something I hadn't experienced before was the approach to learning here. I was used to much more formal teaching: memorising facts, using material from textbooks in essays, things like that. But the way things are done here is much better.

Some people might find it hard to adapt, but I took to it straightaway. (4) The only thing that really took some getting used to was being on first-name terms with tutors and lecturers. That would never have happened with my teachers at school. And the academic staff here are great. I mean, as well as being friendly, they're really professional. They often include the latest research findings in their lectures, and (5) nearly all of them have had textbooks published. So they really are experts in their field.

Someone asked me recently in what way I thought studying here had benefited me most. I thought about it, and replied that throughout my schooldays I was always pretty good at revising and passing exams so that hasn't changed much, but (6) there's been a vast improvement in my problem solving skills.

I will have graduated, I hope, by the end of this year, and I'm meeting my personal tutor on Wednesday to talk about my plans for the future. I know she'd like me to do research work, but (7) I've already made up my mind I'm going to teach locally. I'll be doing that for about a year, I should think.

Sometimes I think back to when I first arrived, and how easy I found it to settle here, but there were certainly a few things that surprised me about living in New Zealand. For instance, I knew it was a long way from Europe, nearly 20,000 kilometres, and I'd already worked out it was almost 10,000 going east to South America. But (8) what I hadn't reckoned on was that it's over 2,000 to Australia, which somehow you'd always thought was close by. And being twelve hours ahead causes its own problems, like when you call someone on their birthday but forget it's the middle of the night over there.

And of course the seasons are the other way round, though right now I'm very happy about the fact that it's nearly summer. My exams started on October 28th and they finish a week from now, which means (9) we're on vacation from November 12th until February 21st. In December in previous years I've gone to Europe to see my family, but to be honest it's not much fun travelling all that way and then finding it's cold and wet when you get there. (10) So I've arranged to spend a few days at a place along the coast from here where you're almost certain to spot whales at that time of the year. I'm really looking forward to it.

> **Exam task answers**
>
> 1 cousin   2 (rock) climbing   3 approach to learning
> 4 first name(s)   5 textbooks   6 problem solving / solving problems   7 teach   8 Australia   9 twelfth/12(th) November / November 12(th) / November (the) twelfth   10 whales

Optional activity

Invite students to talk about a country or countries apart from their own where they would like to study. They can do this as a class or in pairs. Encourage them to consider a range of reasons (including those they have heard on the recording) for studying abroad, and also a number of different countries.

Grammar
Review of future forms

1 This activity can be done in pairs. Give students several minutes to match the verb forms with their uses, and be ready to prompt where necessary with the names of the tenses. Then go through the answers. You may want to elicit examples of the alternative uses (e.g. 3 a prediction based on evidence, *Look at the sky! It's going to rain*) where given.

> **Answers**
>
> 1 c present continuous   2 e future continuous
> 3 d *going to* future   4 a future simple   5 f present simple
> 6 b future perfect

2 You may want to tell the class that four of these sentences are correct. Go through the answers, accepting plausible alternatives, including for the correct sentences, e.g. 5 *I'm going to tell*. You may want to focus on the position of *just* with the future perfect, pointing out that it is the same as with *have just done* in the present perfect.

> **Answers**
>
> 1 arrives   2 *correct; also* will be meeting *or* is going to meet
> 3 I'll have just finished   4 *correct*   5 *correct*   6 I'm going *or* I'm going to go   7 *correct*   8 'll/will go

3 Encourage the use of contracted forms such as *I'll* and *I'm going to* and make sure that students can recognise these forms. You may want to practise the pronunciation. Elicit answers from the class, and if time allows ask them some more questions.

> **Suggested answers**
>
> 2 When are you going to do your homework?
>   I'm going to do it tonight.
> 3 Who are you meeting next weekend?
>   I'm meeting my cousins, on Saturday.
> 4 In which month does the next school term start?
>   It starts in January.
> 5 By what age do you think you will have finished studying?
>   I think I'll have finished by the time I'm 22.
> 6 How many children do you think you will have?
>   I don't think I'll have any.
> 7 Where will you probably be working ten years from now?
>   I'll probably still be working here.

Noun suffixes: *-or, -ist, -ian, -er, -ant*

4 Give students plenty of time to match the suffixes with the groups, using their dictionaries if necessary. Go through the answers, focus on word stress, particularly in group 2

where it falls on the first *i* except in *historian*. Elicit more words to add to groups 3, 4 and 5, e.g. 3 *artist*, *biologist*, *ecologist*; 4 *director*, *decorator*, *contractor*; 5 *teacher*, *designer*, *driver*.

Answers

1 -ant: assistant, (flight) attendant, consultant, accountant, (civil) servant
2 -ian: musician, politician, electrician, historian, mathematician
3 -ist: novelist, guitarist, economist, physicist, psychologist
4 -or: inventor, operator, inspector, investigator, investor
5 -er: dealer, lecturer, banker, philosopher, researcher
Changes
  1 drop the final *e*   2 drop the final *s*, *y* or *ity*   3 drop the final *s*, *cs* or *y*   4 drop the final *e*   5 drop the final *y*, keep the final *e*

5 Explain that the terms *gives* and *receives* are used very broadly here. Model the pronunciation, as the stress changes to the final syllable for the *-ee* ending. Mention or elicit more nouns ending in *-ee*, which may or may not have an equivalent *-er* form, e.g. *escapee*, *mortgagee*, *licensee*.

Answers

the *givers* (or *providers*) are trainer, employer, payer, interviewer, examiner; the *receivers* (or *victims!*) are trainee, employee, payee, interviewee, examinee

6 Go through the list with the class, eliciting the spelling in each case as it may not be apparent from the way the word is pronounced. If there is time, elicit more words by thinking of words ending in these suffixes and giving the class their definitions, as in the exercise.

Answers

1 a participant   2 an instructor   3 a chemist   4 a presenter
5 a specialist   6 a librarian   7 a survivor   8 a motorist
9 a supplier   10 a refugee

Reading and Use of English

Part 7

1 Students discuss the questions as a class or in small groups. Encourage the use of suitable future tenses. The four people are beginning the careers described in the text, but there's no need to mention this yet.

2 Allow a couple of minutes for discussion of these questions, and suggest that students ask themselves these questions whenever they do Reading and Use of English Part 7.

Answers

1 people talking about their careers, four
2 young trainees
3 which person says what about their job, their past and their future

3 Focus attention on the underlined words in question 1, pointing out that these are content words, not grammatical words. Suggest that students do the underlining in pencil in case they want to make changes, or – to avoid them writing in the book or to prepare for the exam – write 1–10 in their

notebooks and then quickly jot down the key words next to each number.

Suggested answers

2 company, bought   3 pleasantly surprised, conditions
4 enthusiasm, determination, success   5 difficult, at first, on time
7 paid, financial, simpler   8 liked, started
9 understand, new things, quickly   10 unsure, how much, will earn

4 Focus attention on the Exam tip and answer any questions students may have about this. Point out that when they read the text, they will be able to compare some of their ideas in Exercise 1 with the four people's predictions for their own futures. Then allow about 20 minutes for the multiple-matching task, in exam conditions.

Exam task answers

1 D   2 C   3 A   4 B   5 C   6 B   7 A   8 B   9 C   10 D

Underlining
A

(3) Before I started here I'd expected to have to work very long hours, but nowadays there's a maximum of 48 hours per week for doctors. There is of course shift work, but the days of junior doctors having to live in and be on call all night are, I was happy to find, long gone.
(7) a clearly laid-down salary structure in this profession, and that makes it easier to think ahead – for instance, if you're intending to take out a loan for house purchase, you know roughly what you'll be able to afford

B

(8) took to the work straightaway
(6) That will mean taking on a lot of added responsibilities such as building lasting business relationships with clients, but I'm sure I'll manage.
(4) If, like me, you're highly motivated, in this firm your career can really take off.

C

(9) there was a tremendous amount to take in all at once
(5) in those early days I had a little trouble meeting deadlines
(2) rumours that a major international corporation is considering taking the firm over

D

(1) I would like to have studied Law at university but I didn't have the grades, so I went straight from school into a law firm.
(10) The salary here is reasonable, although in the present economic climate, with such huge cuts to public spending, that may not be the case for much longer.

5 Allow 30 seconds for students to make sure they have put a letter in every space. Point out that candidates sometimes forget to fill in both spaces on the same line. Go through the answers, eliciting the relevant phrases and sentences.

Phrasal verbs with *take*

6 Explain that the meanings are not in the same order as the verbs in the text. Tell students to study meanings 1–8 and to look at the context for each phrasal verb in the text. Point out that *take on* is used twice, but with different meanings. Go through the answers with the class.

Answers

1 took up   2 taking over   3 taken on   4 took to   5 take in
6 take out   7 take off   8 taking on

7 Students use the phrasal verbs from Exercise 6 to complete the sentences. Go through the answers quickly, possibly eliciting more examples with some or all of the phrasal verbs.

> **Answers**
>
> 1 take on   2 take to   3 taken over   4 taken on   5 taken off
> 6 take up   7 take out   8 take ... in

Extension activity

Divide the class into pairs and give them these instructions:

Imagine you are doing a job that requires a lot of training. Tell your partner about the job, using phrasal verbs with *take*. For example: *Once I'd finished my training, I took up a position in a firm that …*

Speaking

Countable and uncountable nouns

1 This activity could be done in pairs. Allow time for students to read the rules, refer back to the contexts in the Reading and Use of English text and decide on their answers. Check the answers, then elicit more examples of everyday countable and uncountable nouns, e.g. countable: *jobs*, *students*, *lessons*; uncountable: *water*, *air*, *enjoyment*.

> **Answers**
>
> 1 countable nouns   2 uncountable nouns

2 Remind the class that we mainly use *much* and *many* in questions and negative sentences, preferring *a lot* (*of*) or *lots* (*of*) in positive sentences. Point out that the mistakes in these sentences are very common and they include not only plural forms of uncountable nouns, but also incorrect quantifiers like *many*. One sentence requires a change of verb so that it agrees with the number of the noun. Give students five minutes for this, then go through the answers.

> **Answers**
>
> 1 transport   2 a lot of information   3 furniture
> 4 much news *or* a lot of news   5 work   6 a little money
> 7 software   8 some spare time *or* a little spare time *or* a lot
> of spare time   9 unemployment is increasing
> 10 little experience

3 Learning the nouns within the context of a phrase should help students to remember which nouns are uncountable, and avoid mistakes like those in Exercise 2 – many of which may be caused by first language interference. You may want to suggest that students use their dictionaries for some of these, both for meaning and to check whether they are countable. If so, explain that the symbol in the entry is often [C] or [U] after the word *noun*. Go through the answers, pointing out that students will see or hear some of these words in Speaking Part 1 which follows. Explain that there is no singular form of *earnings*, and that it cannot follow a number.

> **Answers**
>
> *countable*: deal, discovery, duty, earnings, institution, opportunity, position, profession, qualification, responsibility
> *uncountable*: advertising, advice, commerce, education, homework, knowledge, leisure, manufacturing, production, research, technology

Part 1

4 🔘 *1.12*   Point out that this is an extract from Part 1 that excludes the introductions at the beginning. Also explain that *media* can be singular or plural, but that it never ends in *-s*. Give the class a few seconds to look at the task, then play the recording once without pausing. Go through the answers and then move on.

> **Answers**
>
> c, e, f

5 🔘 *1.12*   Play the recording once or twice, pausing where necessary, then check the answers. Point out that although one part of the phrase, e.g. *engineering*, *research*, is uncountable, the whole phrase is countable, so the speakers talk about *an engineering course* and *a research degree*. Also highlight the way the speakers expand on the points they make as a good example of how to do Part 1.

> **Answers**
>
> *countable*: (an) engineering course, (a) research degree
> *uncountable*: (some) spare time, (for) pleasure, (doing) overtime, (in) management

> **Recording script**
>
> Examiner: OK, could you tell us something about your family, Alisa?
>
> Alisa: Yes, I live with my mother, who's a scientist, and my younger brother Nikolai. He's starting at the same university as me this September.
>
> Examiner: And your family, Francesco?
>
> Francesco: There's my mother and father, and my two sisters, Giorgia and Sara. They all live at home, but these days I have my own flat.
>
> Examiner: Alisa, what kind of things do you do in your free time?
>
> Alisa: I have to do a lot of homework, but when I have some spare time I like to go to the theatre or a concert. Or I read, at home. Either to increase my knowledge, or just for pleasure. That's what I'll be doing later this evening, actually.
>
> Examiner: And what about your free time, Francesco? What sort of things do you do?
>
> Francesco: I spend quite a lot of time on my computer, reading newspapers in English and looking at interesting websites, things like that. Though sometimes I go out with friends in the evening. If I'm not doing overtime, that is!
>
> Examiner: And what kind of work do you do?

Francesco:	I work in manufacturing. I started out as an ordinary employee, but now I'm in management. I have a lot of responsibilities, but I'm sure there will be some good opportunities in the future if I work hard.
Examiner:	Tell us about your studies, Alisa.
Alisa:	I'm in my second year of an engineering course, and when I graduate I'm going to do a research degree. That's partly because I enjoy studying, but also because these days I think it's very important to get as many qualifications as possible. I'm hoping I'll have finished my studies by the time I'm 26.
Examiner:	OK. Thank you.

6 Make sure that students take turns asking and answering, and that they don't interrupt each other. Monitor pairs for accuracy in the use of future forms, and countable and uncountable nouns.

7 Stress to the class the importance of being diplomatic in their comments and constructive in any criticism.

Reading and Use of English

Part 3

1 This exercise focuses on suffixes students have already seen in Unit 5 Grammar and on the issue of countability. Go through the answers once students have finished, checking spelling. Watch out for plural mistakes in sentences 3, 5, 7 and 8, and ask why *advertisement(s)* is not possible in sentence 8.

> **Answers**
>
> 1 biologist 2 responsibilities 3 production 4 interviewee
> 5 knowledge 6 employers 7 advice 8 advertising
> 9 politicians

2 Set a one-minute time limit, and remind the class to begin every Word Formation task by gist-reading the text. Check the answers and deal with any gist-comprehension difficulties.

> **Suggested answers**
>
> most – medicine and dentistry, least – technology

3 Remind students to look at the example and its context every time they begin Part 3, both as an introduction to the text and as a reminder of what they must do in this task type. Check the answers. Then move on to the exam task. Tell the class that they will have already seen most of the target words in this exam task. You may also want to remind them that more than one change may be necessary in some cases. Allow ten minutes for students working on their own to fill in or note down the answers to the exam task.

> **Answers**
>
> 1 verb 2 noun 3 *-ment* 4 uncountable, no *-s*

> **Exam task answers**
>
> 1 earnings 2 researchers 3 availability 4 qualification
> 5 scientists 6 management 7 consultants 8 engineers

4 Give the class a minute or two to read through the completed text and look at their spelling, then check the answers. Elicit the suffixes used, and ask which of the target nouns are countable, and which are uncountable.

Writing

Part 2 formal letter of application

Optional activity

Discuss with the class the features of formal language. Elicit or give examples of the following:

1 longer words (*extremely* instead of *very*)

2 an impersonal tone (*it has become clear that* instead of *it seems to me*)

3 passive verb forms (*I have been informed* instead of *someone has told me*)

4 few abbreviations (*February* instead of *Feb*)

5 few phrasal verbs (*depart* instead of *set off*)

6 no contracted forms (*I would* instead of *I'd*)

7 long linking phrases (*in view of the fact that* instead of *as*)

8 complete sentences (*Thank you for your reply* instead of *Thanks for writing*)

1 This activity could be done in pairs. Give students a few minutes to study the exam task and note down their answers. Elicit the answers, and suggest that students ask and answer similar questions whenever they do this task type.

> **Answers**
>
> 1 the International Student Fair
> 2 assistants
> 3 giving directions and offering advice
> 4 you must like helping people, have experience of choosing a place of study, and be willing to work evenings
> 5 Ms Ross, in a formal style
> 6 convince her / the organisation that you are suitable for the job

2 Students could underline the phrases and sentences, although in some cases there may be overlap. If you don't want students to write in the book, get them to note down the phrases and sentences. Or, to save time, they could note down just the first and last words of each. Go through the answers with the class, pointing out that many of these phrases are fixed phrases that they can use in future application-writing tasks. You may want to ask students to note these down.

Answers

2 I would like to apply for the post of
3 as advertised in the newspaper on 2 January
4 I have always enjoyed assisting others, I looked at the advantages and disadvantages of many academic institutions, I would be available to work evenings as all my lectures are in the afternoons
5 Could you please tell me how much I would be paid, and whether training would be necessary?
6 last year I worked as a volunteer at a book fair
7 my curriculum vitae, which I enclose
8 If you need any further information, please do not hesitate to contact me.
9 I would be able to attend an interview any morning.

3 Students work on their own for about five minutes. You may want to refer them to the Writing guide on page 91.

4 Allow 35 minutes for the actual writing, as students have already done some preparation and will be given time to check and correct their work in the next exercise.

5 Checking could be done as a peer correction activity, although of course this will not be possible in the exam itself.

Model answer

Dear Ms Ross,

I am writing to apply for the position of assistant at the International Student Fair this summer, as recently advertised in the press.

I have recently begun an undergraduate course in chemistry at the university here, after carefully considering a number of possible higher-education institutions. I therefore feel I have some relevant experience, and I would very much like to pass this on to others.

In addition, over the last twelve months I have done a considerable amount of voluntary work, in particular with inner-city youth groups. I have always felt that the most rewarding kind of job to have is one that involves helping others.

As most of my work with the youth groups took place between 6 and 8 pm I am quite accustomed to working in the evenings. I would, however, be grateful if you could tell me which days and at what times I would be required to work, if I were offered the post.

I enclose my curriculum vitae, and I look forward to receiving your reply.

Yours sincerely,

Maria Karalis

Revision

1 Answers

1 B 2 A 3 D 4 B 5 D 6 C 7 C 8 B

2 Answers

2 little experience 3 few opportunities 4 a little research
5 few professions 6 a little overtime

3 Answers

1 I'll help 2 takes 3 won't mind 4 I'm seeing
5 will have been working 6 I'll be surfing

4 Answers

1 discoveries 2 graduation 3 economist 4 accountant
5 librarian 6 electrician 7 attendant 8 employee

Remind students that there is more practice on the CD-ROM. Also encourage them to do Practice test 1 on the website.

6 Getting better

Unit objectives

TOPICS	health and fitness, sport
GRAMMAR	relative clauses (defining and non-defining), purpose links
VOCABULARY	medical vocabulary, phrasal verbs with *up*, sports vocabulary
READING and USE OF ENGLISH	Part 5: locating answers Part 2: gist-reading, explaining answers
WRITING	Part 2 letter: informal language, purpose links
LISTENING	Part 1: focusing on options
SPEAKING	Part 3: agreeing and politely disagreeing

Reading and Use of English

Medical vocabulary

1 This activity could be done in pairs. Point out that these three categories are quite broad, covering words associated with each heading rather than, for example, types of illness or treatment. Model the pronunciation of words such as *ache*, *bruise* and *wound*, but let partners discuss the meanings first, before checking that everyone has all the words under the correct headings. Elicit verb forms such as *ache*, *bruise* and *injure*, plus *cure*, *cut*, *heal*, *hurt*, *swollen*, etc. Also elicit compounds such as *earache*, *headache*.

> **Answers**
>
> a people: nurse, patient, porter, specialist, surgeon
> b injuries and illnesses: ache, bruise, disease, fever, fracture, graze, infection, pain, sprain, temperature, wound
> c treatment: bandage, injection, medicine, operation, plaster, prescription, stitches, tablets, thermometer

2 Remind the class to focus on minor ailments only, and avoid any conditions that might be embarrassing. Help out where necessary with collocations such as *have an operation, have a temperature, give an injection to (someone), put a bandage on (something), take medicine, take someone's temperature*, etc. Suggest that any students who can't remember having an injury or illness could describe a not-very-serious one suffered by a relative or friend.

3 Explain the meaning of *sight* if necessary. Allow time for students to think about the order of importance of the senses, then note it down. Partners may find they disagree, particularly about the order of *sight*, *hearing* and *touch*.

4 Allow no more than two minutes for this exercise. Point out that there's no specific time given for when Kathy lost her eyesight, but we can infer that it was before birth as she had never experienced colour or shapes. By the end of the text she is able to focus on these, so the answer to the second question is *yes*.

> **Answers**
>
> 1 sight, probably before she was born   2 yes

5 If you prefer students not to write in the book, suggest that they note down the details as shown in the suggested answers below. Remind the class of the importance of focusing on the introductory question, and then looking for what the text says about it. Discourage students from studying every option in detail at this stage, and accept approximate answers when you go through them with the class.

> **Suggested answers**
>
> 2 *from* Dr Percival closed ... *to* ... and stared at the light
> 3 *from* she turned her face away ... *to* ... I don't know what I mean
> 4 *from* Over the next few weeks ... *to* ... how close they were
> 5 *from* But Dr Percival was patient ... *to* ... they worked well

6 Make sure that everyone works on their own. Set a time limit of 15 minutes for the exam task, as students have already read the text through at least twice.

> **Exam task answers**
>
> 1 B   2 A   3 C   4 B   5 C   6 B

7 Give students a couple of minutes to make sure that they have answered every question, and remind them that they lose no marks for guessing incorrectly (this may not be the case in other exams they have taken). If you want students to check together in pairs, allow a little extra time for them to decide who's right if they have different answers. Go through the answers with the class, answering any questions students may have about the language and content of the text.

8 Encourage pairs to discuss pleasant sounds, textures, tastes and smells. When pairs have finished, ask the class which they would enjoy most in each case.

Listening

Part 1

1 Remind students that they should always begin by reading the introductory question and focusing on the key words in it. Although not all these questions will be answered in every introductory question, students will find that many of them are. Give students a minute or two to discuss the questions, then check the answers.

> **Answers**
>
> You hear a woman telling a neighbour in the street about a <u>road accident</u> she has just seen. <u>What happened?</u>
> 1 an event   2 a woman and a neighbour   3 in the street
> 4 to describe the accident   5 very recently

2 Remind students that in every Part 1 question, two of the three possible answers are wrong. Tell them to use the pictures to work out the meanings of *ambulance*, *uninjured* and *first aid*. Check the answers.

Answers

1 C   2 A   3 B

3   ● *2.02*   Advise the class to be careful with the meanings of the past modal and conditional forms that the speaker uses. Then play the recording of the example straight through, without pausing. Don't elicit or give the answer yet.

Recording script

You hear a woman telling a neighbour in the street about a road accident she has just seen.

It all happened so quickly. A car came racing out of that side street without stopping, and the poor cyclist had no chance. He came off and fell onto the road really hard, I thought he must have broken an arm or a leg. I've had some medical training so <u>I would've given him first aid if he'd needed it, but amazingly he didn't, and there didn't seem any point in calling an ambulance, either.</u> The cyclist really told the driver what he thought of him, though, because he could have been badly hurt. And I don't think he would've been able to ride that bike anywhere: it was pretty badly damaged in the crash.

4   Students listen again and identify the relevant parts. Go through the answers with the class, pointing out the way distractors work. Remind students that in the exam there won't be any illustrations of options.

Answers

A: *there didn't seem any point in calling an ambulance, either* – it didn't actually happen
B: *I would've given him first aid if he'd needed it, but amazingly he didn't* – she didn't actually need to give first aid, so we can infer he was not hurt. Plus *I thought he must have broken an arm or a leg* and *he could have been badly hurt*, neither of which were actually the case but could be misunderstood.
C: *I would've given him first aid if he'd needed it*
Correct answer: B

5   Allow plenty of time for this underlining task, and go through the answers once everyone has finished. Tell students to ask themselves these questions every time they do Listening Part 1.

Answers

question 2	*woman*, *street*, *Where*, *now*; 1 place, 2 woman to friend, 3 in the street, 4 no information on *why*, 5 now
question 3	*patient*, *phone*, *What*, *dislike*, *hospital*; 1 opinion/ attitude, 2 patient to someone on the phone, 3 hospital, 4 to complain, 5 no information on *when*
question 4	*two*, *doctor's*, *How*, *feel*, *now*; 1 feelings, 2 two people, 3 doctor's waiting room, 4 to express feelings, 5 now
question 5	*young woman*, *race*, *What*, *agree*; 1 agreement, 2 young woman to friend, 3 to discuss a race, 4/5 no information on *where* or *when*
question 6	*woman*, *phone*, *Why*; 1 purpose, 2 woman to someone on the phone, 3/5 no information on *where* or *when*

6   ● *2.03*   Play the recording straight through, without pausing.

Recording script

You will hear people talking in six different situations. For questions 1–6, choose the best answer (A, B or C).

1   *You overhear a man in a restaurant talking to a colleague about his work.*

The other day I saw a teenager who spends all his time doing sports and he had a whole series of problems: stiff knee, swollen ankles, sore elbow, and so on. I think <u>he expected me to give him painkillers or a prescription</u> for something that would instantly sort everything out, and was obviously disappointed when <u>I told him no such magic cure existed</u>. I suggested instead that he should try doing less training and take a day off each week, as he was clearly overdoing it. It was tricky because many young men in Newtown, where he grew up, are involved in crime. The only ones who aren't are those who are mad about sports, and I didn't want to put him off.

2   *You hear a woman talking to a friend in the street.*

I'm afraid I can't stop long. <u>I've got to pick up something for this evening and they close in half an hour.</u> I was on my way back from seeing Nathan, who's in hospital, and suddenly I remembered <u>there's nothing in the fridge</u> for the kids. They're going into town to see a film that begins at seven and <u>I can't send them off with empty stomachs</u>, so I had to get off the bus a couple of stops early and head this way. Fortunately Nathan is due out of hospital on Monday, which is wonderful news, so tomorrow should be my last visit there.

3   *You hear a patient talking on the phone.*

I know there's a lot in the papers about things going wrong in hospitals, doctors making mistakes and patients catching infections and things like that, but I can't say I have any complaints in that respect. Even the meals they give you aren't as bad as everyone says, certainly no worse than what I cook for myself at home! <u>I would like a bit more peace and quiet, though. There always seems to be something going on 24/7, and in a place like this sound travels a long way.</u> Still, the nurses say I should be out of here by the weekend, so I'll soon be back at the house.

4   *You overhear two people talking in a doctor's waiting room.*

Man: Actually I was here last week after my daughter's pet rabbit bit me.
Woman: Really? I thought rabbits were supposed to be friendly animals.
Man: Me too, until Bunny sank his teeth into my arm. When I told a friend of mine about it he couldn't stop laughing, but I didn't really see the funny side of it and I got a bit cross with him at the time.
Woman: And what did the doctor do?
Man: She gave me an injection and told me to come back if there were any signs of infection, <u>but so far there haven't been, I'm glad to say</u>. I've kept away from Bunny, though, just in case he gets nasty again.

5   *You hear a young woman talking to a friend about a cross-country race.*

Man: My knee still hurts, and I've got that cross-country race coming up in two weeks.

Exam task answers

1 B   2 C   3 B   4 C   5 A   6 A

7 Give the class a minute to make sure that they have answered all the questions, and remind them that they lose no marks for guessing incorrectly. If you want students to check together in pairs, allow a little extra time for them to decide who's right if they have different answers. Go through the answers, answering any questions students may have about content or language.

Grammar

Phrasal verbs with *up*

1 Give the class a minute to look at the extracts, then elicit the answers.

Answers

grew up means 'became an adult', *coming up* means 'getting nearer in time', *cleared up* means 'got better'

Optional activity

Point out that one reason native speakers understand phrasal verbs – including newly coined ones – is that they are aware of these patterns of meaning, so it is useful for learners to become familiar with them, too. Elicit more examples of phrasal verbs with *up* that have each of these general meanings:

1 in an upward direction, e.g. *get up*, *stand up*

2 increasing, improving or approaching, e.g. *build up*, *dress up*, *walk up*

3 completing, e.g. *breakup*, *end up*

2 This activity could be done in pairs, students completing the sentences and matching the phrasal verbs with their meanings at the same time. Check answers, and then

present or elicit more phrasal verbs with *up*, e.g. *beat up*, *bring up*, *catch up*, *cheer up*, *do up*, *drink up*, *drive up*, *fill up*, *give up*, *jump up*, *light up*, *lock up*, *make up*, *pull up*, *save up*, *shoot up*, *tear up*, *tighten up*.

Answers

1 eat, d   2 use, j   3 tidy, i   4 speak, b   5 speed, c
6 split, a   7 healed, h   8 ran, g   9 dug, f   10 sum, e

Relative clauses

3 Give the class plenty of time to study the pairs of sentences, if necessary suggesting they refer to the Grammar reference on page 108. Then go through the answers, focusing on each pair of sentences in turn. You may want to elicit further examples of both kinds of relative clause and the difference in meaning between them. Point out that omission of the relative pronoun is only possible in defining relative clauses, and never with *whose*.

Answers

1 b only has one sister, a has more than one
2 b had never seen a match before, a had only seen boring matches before
3 *which* could be left out in a because it is a defining relative clause, and the relative pronoun is the object of the clause

4 Allow students a little time to study all the sentences again and look at the Grammar reference. Then elicit the answers.

Answers

1 defining   2 non-defining   3 non-defining; immediately before the relative pronoun, and possibly also at the end of the relative clause

5 Explain, if necessary, that students will need to make a small change to the second sentence – begin it with a relative pronoun and put it in commas – then add the rest of the first sentence. Go through the answers.

Answers

2 , which was set in a school, was
3 , when the World Cup was held in South Africa, Spain
4 , who were in an accident,
5 , whose mother had also been a top swimmer, won a medal
6 , where the final was about to take place, everyone was

6 Point out that there is just one mistake in each sentence, apart from one sentence in which two commas need to be inserted. Go through the answers with the class, asking why students think the candidates made these mistakes.

Answers

1 which   2 *comma before* which, Davos   3 when, June
4 who/that, people   5 whose, man   6 *commas before* who *and saw*, Mark   7 where, a gym

Speaking

Sports vocabulary

1 This activity could be done in pairs. Once students have done the matching task, check the answers. Point out that we often use these expressions as compound nouns:

football pitch, *ski slope*, *tennis court*, etc. Then elicit more sports played in each place, e.g. *badminton court*.

Answers

course – golf
court – basketball, squash, tennis
gym – gymnastics
pitch – baseball, football, hockey, rugby
ring – boxing
rink – ice skating
sea – diving, sailing, surfing
slope – skiing, snowboarding
track – athletics, cycling, motorcycling

2 This activity also presents a set of sports vocabulary. If students don't know any of these words, get them to use their dictionaries. Make sure that everyone has the correct answer and spelling, and elicit more examples, e.g. *horse rider*, *racing driver*.

Suggested answers

do – athletics (athlete), boxing (boxer), gymnastics (gymnast)
play – baseball (baseball player), basketball (basketball player), football (football player *or* footballer), golf (golfer), hockey (hockey player), rugby (rugby player), squash (squash player), tennis (tennis player)
go – cycling (cylist), diving (diver), ice skating (ice skater), motorcycling (motorcyclist), sailing (sailor), skiing (skier), snowboarding (snowboarder), surfing (surfer)

3 Encourage students to use their dictionaries if they have any difficulties with the vocabulary. Check the answers and possibly elicit the names for more items, e.g. *hockey stick*.

Suggested answers

A baseball player uses a (baseball) bat.
A surfer uses a (surf)board.
A golfer uses a (golf) club.
A boxer wears (boxing) gloves.
A motorcyclist wears a helmet.
A tennis player uses a (tennis) racket.
An ice skater wears (ice) skates.
A skier uses skis.

Agreeing and politely disagreeing

4 2.04 Play the recording several times and choral drill. Point out the importance of correct intonation, particularly when disagreeing politely.

Recording script

Man: I think you're probably right.
Man: I don't think so. My own feeling is ...

5 2.05 Allow a few minutes for the class to complete the expressions. Play the recording so that students can check their answers, go through the answers and then get students working in pairs to practise saying the expressions to each other. Monitor for correct pronunciation.

Recording script

Agreeing
a   Yes, you're absolutely right.
b   I think so, too.
c   Yes, I agree with that.
d   That's just what I was thinking.
Politely disagreeing
e   Perhaps, but what about ...?
f   I'm not so sure. Don't you think ...?
g   I don't know about that.
h   I'm not really so keen on ...

Answers

a absolutely   b so   c agree   d just   e what   f sure
g know   h keen

Part 3

6 2.06 Explain that this task is similar to Speaking Part 3, although it does not take place in exam conditions. Play the recording once, then elicit the answers. Point out that it isn't necessary, either in this activity or in the exam, for students to reach the same decision at the end. The important thing is the discussion, not the outcome.

Answers

1 gymnastics   2 motorcycling   3 rugby, snowboarding
4 boxing

7 2.06 Play the recording once or twice more and give students time to write down the phrases they hear. Check the answers.

Answers

1 c   2 g   3 d   4 a   5 f   6 b   7 e
The speakers do not use h.

Recording script

Teacher: Now, I'd like you to talk about something together for about two minutes. Here are some sports that can be dangerous. Look at the task and talk to each other about what can happen to people doing these sports if they are not careful. You now have some time to look at the task. *[15-second pause]*
Could you start now, please?

Tomasz: Is it OK if we start with rugby?

Eva: Yes, let's begin with that.

Tomasz: Well, I think you have to be very careful in this sport, because it's quite violent and they don't have any protection like in American football.

Eva: (c) <u>Yes, I agree with that.</u> They don't wear a helmet to protect their head, so they can have some serious injuries. Also to their arms and legs.

Tomasz: It's the same for the motorcycling. Even though they wear a helmet and some body protection, it's still very dangerous if they fall off when they're going fast.

Eva: It's much more dangerous than car racing, I think. The drivers are a lot safer because of the way they make the cars these days, but if you crash a motorbike you will probably still get injured.

Tomasz: And what about diving? What can happen there?

Eva: Well, when you're deep in the water I suppose the biggest risk is that for some reason you can't breathe. Such as getting trapped under the water and your air runs out. Or something goes wrong with the oxygen thing.

Tomasz: Or a shark attacks you. That's another danger.

Eva: (g) I don't know about that. In films, maybe. But it's not very common in real life, is it? Anyway, let's go on to the next one.

Tomasz: Yes, gymnastics. Now that's definitely not as dangerous as some of the others. I mean, even if you're really careless, normally the worst thing that can happen is that you get hurt a bit, nothing very bad.

Eva: (d) That's just what I was thinking, really. It can't be very nice if you fall, but at least the ground is soft. It's not like landing on a racetrack, or even a rugby pitch.

Tomasz: Though people can get hurt snowboarding, and they do that on snow, which is pretty soft. Probably because they go so fast.

Eva: Especially if they go off the proper slopes. If they do that in bad weather they can't see where they're going, and they can hit a tree, or rocks.

Tomasz: I suppose hitting rocks is the biggest risk for people who go surfing, too. They might be just under the surface but you don't know until a wave pushes you onto them.

Eva: (a) Yes, you're absolutely right. I think you have to know the place where you are going surfing, to make sure there aren't any dangerous ones near you. And always have a surfing buddy with you, someone who knows where you are all the time.

Tomasz: Yes, that makes it much safer.

Eva: Next there's boxing. What do you think of that? To me it's not really a sport – it's just fighting, hitting someone's head. That's really stupid, and it must damage them in the end.

Tomasz: (f) I'm not so sure. Don't you think that wearing gloves makes it safer?

Eva: Well, actually last week I read that boxers hit each other much harder with gloves on, because without them they would hurt their hands.

Teacher: Thank you. Now you have a minute to decide which two are the most dangerous sports.

Tomasz: Shall I start?

Eva: Yes, go on.

Tomasz: OK. So which two of these sports do we think are the most dangerous? I'd say the motorcycling simply because it's so fast and the surface is so hard.

Eva: (b) I think so, too. And also boxing. They should ban it completely, starting with the next Olympic Games. Don't you agree that it's one of the most dangerous sports in the world?

Tomasz: (e) Perhaps, but what about rugby? Or snowboarding?

Eva: Boxing.

Tomasz: OK, we have different opinions about this, but let's leave it at that.

Eva: Yes, that's fine.

Teacher: Thank you.

8 Allow about three minutes for students to do the task. Remind students to begin the discussion by saying something like *Would you like to start, or shall I?* Also remind them of the importance of taking turns and responding to what the other person says. If necessary, help out with any key vocabulary such as *climbing* or *snowboarding*.

9 This discussion could be carried out by pairs forming larger groups, by mingling with others, or as a brief class discussion.

Reading and Use of English

Part 2

1 Divide the class into pairs. If necessary, prompt with suggestions such as *putting up information signs*, or pointing out that volunteers normally aren't paid. This discussion task should be done quickly, as the aim is to set up reasons for reading the text.

2 Allow 90 seconds at most for students to read the text, and quickly elicit some answers from the class.

Answers

jobs – checking tickets, handing out uniforms, showing spectators to their seats, tidying after events have finished
advantages – helping to make the Games a success for everyone, training (though may not be paid)
disadvantages – unpaid, no accommodation, no travel expenses, giving up two weeks of their summer holidays, spending three days being trained

3 Refer the class to the Exam tip and allow 10–12 minutes for students to write their answers (they have already read through the text).

Exam task answers

1 whose 2 who 3 which 4 own 5 where 6 from 7 up
8 that *or* which

4 Students, in pairs, discuss the answers to the exam task. Go through the answers with the class. Point out the use of *give up*, which usually means 'stop doing (often something harmful)', but here means 'to do without part of one's holidays in order to do something else' (*up* has the sense of 'completely'). With a strong class, ask students to explain the use of phrasal verbs and relative pronouns in items 1, 2, 3, 5, 7 and 8.

Writing

Purpose links

1 Check the answers, and if there are any difficulties, elicit more examples by giving the beginnings of sentences and asking the class to complete them, e.g. *This morning I turned on the radio …* (*to / in order to / so as to hear the news*).

2 Point out that there are several possibilities in each case, but one answer using each structure is enough. When students have finished, encourage them to think of similar questions to ask each other.

Part 2 letter

3 Allow students a minute to study the instructions and answer the questions. Then go through the answers with the class, suggesting that students ask themselves questions like these every time they do a Writing Part 2 letter task.

4 Deal with questions 1 and 2 separately, allowing only a minute for students to answer gist-question 1 before moving on to the more detailed reading required in question 2.

5 Refer the class back to the the Quick steps and Exam tip for Writing Part 2 informal letter in Unit 1, and to the Writing guide on page 90. Then allow a few minutes for planning.

6 Give the class no more than 30 minutes for the actual writing, bearing in mind that they have already spent time studying the input material and planning their work, and then allow another five minutes for checking. Encourage the use of both kinds of purpose link and relative clause.

Revision

1 | **Answers**

Across

1 pitch   3 track   7 sailor   9 ache   11 nurse   12 bruise
14 court   16 patient   17 course

Down

2 helmet   4 athlete   5 fracture   6 sprain   7 sight
8 cyclist   10 wound   12 bat   13 slope   15 ring

2 | **Answers**

2 , when I was born, ... who *or* that
3 whose ... that *or* which
4 where ... who *or* that
5 whose ... that *or* which
6 who *or* that ... , which
You can leave out *that* or *which* in sentence 5, and *who* or
that in sentence 6.

3 | **Answers**

1 order   2 who *or* that   3 if   4 whose   5 which   6 same
7 to   8 so

4 | **Answers**

1 in order that it   2 who grew up   3 so as not to get *or* so
that he didn't / did not get   4 up the rubbish that was *or*
which was   5 in order not to   6 whose name is

Remind students that there is more practice on the CD-ROM.

7 Green issues

Unit objectives

TOPICS	the environment, the weather
GRAMMAR	review of conditionals 1–3, mixed conditionals, comparison of adjectives and adverbs, contrast links phrases with *in*
VOCABULARY	
READING and	Part 6: text organisation, reference words, linking expressions
USE OF ENGLISH	Part 4: focusing on grammatical changes
WRITING	Part 1 essay: contrast links, for and against
LISTENING	Part 3: taking care with conditional forms
SPEAKING	Part 2: comparing using *-er*, *more* and *(not) as/so … as*

Listening

Part 3

1 The matching task could be done by eliciting the pairs of words and the answers from the class, or in small groups. Answer any questions that students may have about meaning or get students to look up the expressions in their dictionaries. Make sure that everyone links the pairs either by drawing a line between them, or by noting them down in their vocabulary notebooks. Discuss whether each thing is good or harmful for the environment, ensuring everyone understands what is involved in each case.

Answers

acid rain, animal conservation, carbon emissions, climate change, global warming, industrial waste, melting icecaps, oil spills, renewable resources, solar power
good – animal conservation, renewable resources, solar power
harmful – acid rain, carbon emissions, climate change, global warming, industrial waste, melting icecaps, oil spills

2 Get students to use their dictionaries, if necessary, to check some of the meanings, and briefly discuss each weather condition. Then ask the class which conditions are shown in the photos (see **Answers**). This activity introduces the topic of the Listening text, and students will hear these four expressions on the recording. You may also want to elicit or present other words for extreme conditions, such as *hurricane*, *typhoon*, *tropical cyclone*, *blizzard*.

Answers

1 heatwave   2 extreme rainfall   3 tropical storm   4 tornado

3 Allow only a minute for students to identify the topic, then elicit the answer.

Suggested answer

extreme weather events the speakers have seen, and what happened

4 Give students about five minutes to underline the key words, then elicit some answers.

Suggested answers

A injured, going on (during, at the same time)
B glad, by train (pleased, disappointed; rail)
C swim, safety (water, drown; escape, danger)
D stayed, all the time (didn't move, watched; throughout, during)
E help people, while (gave, offered; during, at the same time)
F fortunate, found, shelter (lucky, just as well; discovered, came across; safety, protection)
G more severe, previous years (worse, stronger; summer before)
H wasn't sure, do (didn't know, wasn't used to; go, run)

5 Focus attention on the Quick steps, then on this sentence spoken by the first speaker students will hear. Make sure that everyone understands *shelter* and elicit the full forms of *would've* (*would have*) and *wasn't* (*was not*). Give students, working in pairs, a minute to discuss the question. Then ask the class for the answer, and the reason. Stress the importance of being careful with hypothetical statements in Part 3, and in other parts of the Listening test, when questions are testing comprehension of factual information.

Answer

no, because Speaker 1's sentence refers to something that didn't happen, with imaginary results, whereas F describes a real event

6 🔘 *2.07* Play the recording without pausing, in exam conditions.

Note: the speakers use a range of conditional forms which will be used as examples in Grammar that follows.

Recording script

You will hear five different people talking about extreme weather events that they have seen. For questions 1–5, choose from the list (A–H) what each speaker says about what happened. Use the letters only once. There are three extra letters which you do not need to use.

Speaker 1

It was a fine spring day and I was out walking in the fields, when suddenly everything went dark and I noticed this dark column in the sky. It seemed to be getting bigger and then I realised it was a tornado, heading my way. I'd seen them on TV, of course, but there'd never been one round here so this wasn't something I was used to. If there had been shelter around I would've used it, but there just wasn't any. Then hailstones and bits of rubbish started to fall around me, so I just ran, anywhere. The tornado came closer and closer, but at the very last moment it turned left. If it hadn't changed direction, I wouldn't be here now.

Speaker 2

The forecast had mentioned extreme rainfall, but <u>I'd heard that before in June and it usually meant that everything got very wet and that was about it. But this time it just kept pouring down, hour after hour.</u> I knew that if the river reaches a certain level it bursts its banks, so I walked up through the village. That was a mistake, because I suddenly saw this mass of water and mud racing down the main street towards me. If I'd stayed there I would've been in big trouble, so I turned and ran, desperately looking for shelter. Through shop windows I saw terrified people, but the doors were closed and I had to keep running until I was out of the village. I was unhurt, but if it happened again, I'd find somewhere safe much sooner.

Speaker 3

So far this year we've had hardly any rainfall, and unless it rains soon, most of the crops will die. As they did last year, when the same thing happened. We had a heatwave in May that left the countryside dry as a bone, and not surprisingly there have been bush fires, including one right here. <u>From my upstairs window I saw the smoke in the distance, and then watched, horrified, as the flames came closer and closer, before thankfully stopping just short of my house.</u> Some people were trapped in a valley near here, and there could've been a tragedy if they hadn't found a cave where they could shelter until the worst of the fire had passed. They had a few minor burns, but were otherwise none the worse for their experience.

Speaker 4

We'd had a very mild winter on the island, with just the occasional sea mist and nothing stronger than light breezes. Then one evening the wind started to pick up, and huge waves began crashing onto the beach, until by midnight it was clear we were being hit by a tropical storm. From my house I saw a large tree fall onto the street, and a car crash into it. I dashed outside to help, but as I got close I saw the driver and passenger had had a lucky escape and could manage on their own. By then there were branches flying everywhere, so I ran back indoors, avoiding all but one of them on the way. <u>I had some cuts and bruises</u>, but it might've been a lot worse if it'd been a bigger branch.

Speaker 5

We'd had days of freezing temperatures last month, with frost on the car windows every morning, but I'd decided to drive home for Christmas anyway. All went well until the mountain pass, when a snowstorm suddenly struck. Within minutes some vehicles were in trouble, unable to go any further uphill. And I was stuck behind them. If I had a bigger car, I could have slept in it. But it's tiny and I'm very tall. So it was a miserable, sleepless night, even though I had several blankets with me. Actually, <u>I got out and offered a couple to the family in the car behind and they were very grateful for them</u>, which was nice. But I know one thing for sure: if I have to travel next Christmas, I'll take the train.

> **Exam task answers**
>
> 1 H   2 G   3 D   4 A   5 E

7 Once everyone has made sure that they have chosen a letter for all the questions, go through the answers with the class.

Optional activity

Invite students to talk about any extreme kinds of weather they have experienced. Ask them what they would do in the situations described in the recording. Encourage the use of vocabulary from Exercise 2, but not full conditional forms at this stage. Ask the class for some brief anecdotes and suggestions for what to do, then move on.

Grammar

Review of conditionals 1–3

1 This activity could be done in pairs. Give students plenty of time to answer the questions, then go carefully through each one, ensuring that everyone notes down the correct answer. Point out that the order of the clauses can be reversed, and that modal verbs such as *can*, *may* and *could* can be used instead of *will* and *would* in the other conditional forms, too.

> **Answers**
>
> a simple present, *will* future   b past simple, *would* + infinitive   c past perfect, *would* + *have* + past participle
> a no, likely   b unlikely, no   c no, no

2 Suggest that pairs or students working on their own use the verb forms as the main clues, referring back to their answers in Exercise 1 for the rules. Go through the answers, making sure that everyone understands the meaning in each case. If time allows, elicit more possible endings to some or all of the sentences, using the same conditional form.

> **Answers**
>
> 1 c first   2 e third   3 b second   4 a first   5 d second

3 Allow a couple of minutes for students working on their own or in pairs to correct the mistakes, then check the answers. Ask the class for other common mistakes with conditionals, particularly those made by students of their own first language(s).

> **Answers**
>
> 1 I would try   2 I would have written   3 If I lived   4 we will have
> 5 I would spend   6 If I had known

4 Students complete the questions as a written exercise. Depending on the level of the class, you may want to elicit the correct question forms first. Then encourage pairs to answer with as many sentences as possible. Elicit some answers when they have finished, highlighting the possible variations in full and contracted forms, and *were able to* and *could* in question 3. Also point out that the order of clauses could be reversed.

Mixed conditionals

5 Students may well have already noticed in their general reading and listening that English actually uses a variety of combinations of verb tenses in conditional sentences, but – depending on the level of your class – you could point out that the rules of grammar are sometimes oversimplified at lower levels. You may also want to mention other combinations that fall outside the *conditionals 1–3* patterns, e.g. *I'll do the shopping if you'll cook; You must be tired if you've been working all day; If you've spent all that money already, I'm not going to give you any more*, and – with a strong class – elicit more. Go through the examples and the answers with the class.

6 Point out that the sentences all require either a past perfect form, or present or past conditional form, and that most of these will be negative. Allow a couple of minutes for students working on their own or in pairs to write their answers, then check.

7 Give prompts from the suggested answers if necessary, then monitor to ensure that pairs use full sentences accurately.

Reading and Use of English

Part 6

1 Ask the class these questions, extending the scope to include other electronic goods such as microwaves and TVs.

2 Point out that identifying sections of the text that deal with different aspects of the topic can be a useful general indication of where particular sentences are likely to go. Allow two minutes for this 'top down' reading activity, then elicit the answer.

3 Give students a minute to underline only words likely to link elsewhere, not within a particular sentence, e.g. *their* in sentence B. Get students to note down the linking words if you don't want them to write in the book. You may want to go through the answers now, or – with a stronger class – leave that until students have completed the exam task.

4 Allow no more than 20 minutes for the class to do the exam task, working alone.

5 Give the class a few extra minutes to make sure that they have chosen one letter for every question, but point out that in the exam they would need to do this very quickly. Then go through the answers, focusing attention on the linking and reference words and how they match each other.

6 Remind the class to look for vocabulary links such as synonyms whenever they do Reading and Use of English Part 6. Encourage them to use the context to work out the meanings of these words, but allow them to use dictionaries for any that they find particularly difficult. Point out that some of the words, e.g. *substances*, appear elsewhere in the text, giving further contextual clues. Elicit the meanings of these mainly B2-level words and phrases.

7 Give students a few minutes to find these mainly B2-level words, then go through the answers. There are more B2-level expressions in the text that you may wish to focus on: *controversial* (4), *aware* (4), *key* (5), *principle* (5), *producer* (5), *dealers* (5), *finance* (5), *network* (5), *council* (5), *feature* (5), *establish* (6).

> **Answers**
>
> a devices   b chimneys   c hi-tech   d regulation   e recycling
> f generate   g greenhouse gas   h chemicals   i disposal
> j processed

Optional activity

Students add to their vocabulary notebooks the words and phrases from Exercises 6 and 7 that they think they are most likely to need to use in the future.

Speaking

Comparative forms

1 This section focuses on comparatives only, as they are particularly relevant to Speaking Part 2. For superlatives, refer the class to the Grammar reference on page 109. Allow students working in pairs a couple of minutes to complete the summary, then make sure that everyone has completed it correctly.

> **Answers**
>
> 1 than   2 as   3 so   4 less

2 Point out that the comparative forms practised here will be useful in Speaking Part 2. Allow a couple of minutes for the class to write their answers, then check.

> **Answers**
>
> 2 less hard than these
> 3 harmful as the old ones
> 4 less successfully than big companies *or* worse than big
>   companies
> 5 as sensible as the second (one) *or* as sensible as the other
>   one
> 6 so negatively as driving a car *or* as negatively as driving a car

Part 2

3 Draw attention to the Quick steps. You may want to tell students not to worry if the examiner stops them: this is normal when the minute is up. Pairs look quickly at the photos, as this is not the exam task. Elicit the features, without letting them make any comparisons at this stage, and then move on.

4 Pairs focus on the instructions but not the photos. Give them a minute, then check the answers.

> **Answers**
>
> In task 1, A has to compare the photographs and say what they think could be good or bad about living there. B has to say which place they would prefer to live in.
> In task 2, B has to say why they think people have chosen to take part in these activities. A has to say which of the activities will do more to help the environment.

5 Refer the class to the Quick steps, which include advice on using the grammar from the previous section in Part 2. Suggest that in Exam task 1 Candidate B should do the time-keeping, and remind B to spend about 20 seconds answering their question, giving a reason or example. Monitor pairs, ensuring that the non-speaker does not interrupt until the 60 seconds are up.

Partners now change roles and discuss the photos in the same way. Encourage them to vary the language used, not copy what their partner said.

6 You may want students to comment only on their own speaking, or on their partner's speaking, too. If they're commenting on their partner's performance, advise them to be diplomatic and constructive. You might also suggest that they comment on each other's use of the target comparatives.

Reading and Use of English

Phrases with *in*

1 This activity could be done in pairs. Encourage students to use the context to work out the meaning of each of these useful B2-level phrases. They should be able to get at least an idea of what each phrase means, and then find an expression (a–j) which is similar. Go through the answers, eliciting more examples with each target phrase if there is time.

> **Answers**
>
> 1 i   2 d   3 e   4 c   5 a   6 j   7 b   8 f   9 h   10 g

2 Explain that students should use eight of the ten expressions with *in* to complete the text. Check the answers.

> **Answers**
>
> 1 in progress   2 play a part in   3 In practice   4 in due course
> 5 in all   6 in doubt   7 In the meantime   8 in the long term

Part 4

3 Focus attention on the example, give the class 30 seconds to answer the questions and then elicit the answers.

> **Answers**
>
> 1 present simple + infinitive becomes second conditional, *your*
>   becomes *my*
> 2 *my* job = 1 mark, *if I were* = 1 mark: each of the two phrases
>   gets one mark when correctly formed

4 Tell students that they only need to identify the main structures, not study the sentences in detail for secondary changes. Give them no more than two minutes, then go briefly through the answers. Suggest that students identify the main change every time they begin a Part 4 task.

> **Answers**
>
> 1 conditional (third)   2 comparative adverb   3 phrase with *in*
> 4 conditional (third)   5 phrase with *in*
> 6 conditional (third)   7 comparative adjective
> 8 conditional (mixed)

Students do the exam task individually, either writing the words in the book or noting down just the missing words, not the whole sentence.

> **Exam task answers**
>
> 1 would've / would have called | if I   2 drive so well | as
> 3 aren't / are not | in favour   4 would have / would've /
> 'd have arrived | in   5 probably not as | harmful as
> 6 would work | if we'd / we had

5 Give the class a minute to check for content and language accuracy, then go through the answers, pointing out which words in each score a mark.

Writing

Contrast links

1 Tell the class to look at the Grammar reference on page 109, and give them a couple of minutes to do this. Depending on the level of your class, you may want to explain that expressions like *nevertheless* are followed by a comma, and *despite* by a noun or gerund. Go through the answers, possibly giving or eliciting more examples with each. Point out that some, but not all, of these linking expressions can be used at the beginning or middle of a sentence, Also draw students' attention to *On the one hand* in sentence 6, which often begins the first clause in a sentence containing a contrast.

> **Answers**
>
> 1 Even though   2 whereas   3 In contrast,
> 4 Despite the fact that   5 Despite   6 On the other hand,

Part 1 essay

2 Give the class 30 seconds to study the questions, then elicit the answers, without going into the reasons for their agreement or disagreement (question 4).

> **Answers**
>
> 1 the class has done a project on the environment
> 2 the teacher
> 3 whether we are doing enough to protect our world

3 Allow students working in pairs lots of time to study the model essay and note down their answers. Then go through these with the class. Answer any other language questions students may have.

> **Answers**
>
> 1 yes – it's a little over the maximum but this normally doesn't
>   matter, yes
> 2 1 d   2 e   3 b   4 c, a
> 3 a Despite, in contrast, On the other hand, Nevertheless
>   b Firstly, In addition
>   c *we should do more ... if we really want* (modal conditional),
>   *unless richer nations give up ... our planet will in the long
>   term face* (first conditional)
>   d the problems are getting worse, do more than just talk, we
>   use more ... than ever before, lead a greener way of life,
>   unless richer nations

4 Students work alone and practise brainstorming ideas for their own essay. It's probably best not to elicit answers.

5 Give students, working on their own, a few minutes to choose and make a plan.

6 Allow no more than 35 or 40 minutes for writing as students have already studied the task. Remind them to leave at least five minutes of that time for checking, which could be done as a peer correction activity.

> **Model answer**
>
> We are often told that we must do more to look after the environment, that the Earth will be damaged forever unless we take steps now to save it. But how true is this?
>
> First of all, there can be no doubt that the rapidly increasing numbers of cars, factories and houses are polluting our towns and countryside. In addition, growing populations consuming more products are using more and more of the Earth's scarce resources and, at the same time, are creating huge amounts of waste.
>
> Nevertheless, people's greater awareness of the dangers means that we are now turning to alternative, cleaner forms of energy such as wave power. Moreover, in our personal lives we are recycling more instead of throwing things out, using less electricity and starting to go by bicycle instead of by car. Technology, too, is playing a part, as homes become greener and electric vehicles a reality.
>
> To sum up, although the increasing pressure on the environment is certainly a challenge, I believe that we are now beginning to respond to it successfully.

Revision

1 | **Answers**

1 than   2 further/farther   3 more   4 as   5 as   6 far *or* much
7 less   8 so *or* as   9 as   10 less

2 | **Answers**

1 B   2 B   3 B   4 C   5 A   6 A   7 C   8 D

3 | **Suggested answers**

1 Where will you go next summer if it's very hot? I'll go to the seaside if it's very hot.
2 What would you most like to see if you went to Antarctica? If I went to Antarctica, I'd most like to see the penguins.
3 If it had snowed last month, would you have gone skiing then? No, if it'd snowed last month, I wouldn't have gone skiing then.
4 What will happen to the rainforests if we don't protect them? The rainforests will no longer exist if we don't protect them.
5 If you didn't have any electronic items, would you miss them? Yes, if I didn't have any electronic items, I'd miss them.
6 Do you think you would have done better in your last exam if you had revised more? No, I don't think I would've done better in my last exam if I'd revised more.
7 What would life be like today if we hadn't invented the car? Life would be much more pleasant today if we hadn't invented the car.

4 | **Answers**

1 quite so dirty | as   2 if we | hadn't / had not eaten
3 in | the long term   4 I'd / I had remembered | to take
5 if | I were you
6 if | they hadn't / had not helped *or* had | they not helped

---

Remind students that there is more practice on the CD-ROM.

Unit objectives

TOPICS	science, technology
GRAMMAR	review of passive forms, articles
VOCABULARY	communications vocabulary, science vocabulary, collocations
READING and USE OF ENGLISH	Part 5: reference, exemplification, meaning from context
	Part 1: identifying collocations
WRITING	Part 2 article: reason and result links
LISTENING	Part 2: focusing on numbers
SPEAKING	Part 4: adding points, involving the reader

Reading and Use of English

Communications vocabulary

1 This activity could be done in pairs. Make sure that everyone understands the terms, if necessary giving examples such as Facebook or Skype, then elicit the answers from the class. Have a brief class discussion on the popularity of each form of communication and which students use, and make a note of their general preferences – this could be useful to know when setting project work and other assignments.

> **Answers**
>
> 1 emailing   2 blogging   3 instant messaging   4 texting
> 5 social networking   6 video conferencing

2 Explain that compound nouns may be two nouns or, for example, an adjective or verb + noun. Students note down the compound nouns in their vocabulary notebooks and say which means of electronic communication each is associated with, although increasingly the answer is likely to be *both* for most of them. Check the answers, ensuring that the meaning of every word is clear. Point out that for a mobile phone we say *keypad*.

> **Answers**
>
> computer: bookmark, broadband, database, desktop, keyboard, spreadsheet, website
> mobile phone: handset, ringtones
> both: password

3 Either ask the class these questions, or get pairs to discuss them briefly.

Part 5

4 Give the class no more than two minutes to read the text, then elicit the answer. Suggest that students take the same approach whenever they read a text that has a question about the topic in the title.

> **Suggested answer**
>
> In some particular ways it has driven people apart, but overall it has brought the world closer together.

5 Allow students only a minute to do the identification task, then quickly go through the answers. Encourage students always to notice the types of question as they skim through them at the beginning.

> **Answers**
>
> a 4   b 3   c 1

6 Tell students to work on their own for 15 minutes. Remind them to refer to the Quick steps as they do questions 1, 3 and 4.

> **Exam task answers**
>
> 1 B   2 C   3 A   4 D   5 D   6 C

7 Give students a couple of minutes to make sure that they have answered every question, and remind them that they lose no marks for guessing incorrectly (this may not be the case in other exams they have taken). If you want students to check together in pairs, allow a little extra time for them to decide who's right if they have different answers. To do this, they could discuss why the other three options are wrong before making a final decision. Go through the answers with the class, answering any questions students may have about the language and content of the text.

8 Give students a few minutes to discuss a few of the points made by the writer. If necessary, prompt by mentioning his views on free online newspapers or music downloads, digital multi-tasking, the potential for misunderstandings in emails, whether we would really miss the Internet if it disappeared, etc. Remind the class that the correct answers to the multiple-choice questions summarise many of the main points of the text.

Listening

Science vocabulary

1 If time allows, begin by asking the class *How useful is a basic knowledge of science in everyday life?* and prompting a brief discussion, with examples. Then focus attention on the words and answer any questions students may have about them. Depending on the first language(s) of the class, most of these words (possibly excluding *breakthrough* and *test tubes*) may be cognates. Then tell students to do the quiz on their own. Don't go through the answers yet.

2 🔊 2.08 Play the recording once, make sure that everyone has the right answers, then read out this light-hearted assessment to the class.

Score 1 mark for each correct answer.

Score 0–6: Your score isn't the greatest, but it's never too late to learn. It's time for double science lessons, with lots of homework!

Score 7–12: That Nobel Prize is a long way off. You have some basic knowledge, but you really need to get those science textbooks out again.

Score 13–18: Well done. You either remember the science you did at school, or you're still studying it. Though of course there's still much more to learn.

Recording script

1 Biology is the study of living things.

2 Chemistry is the study of substances and how they react or combine with each other.

3 Physics is the study of matter and energy, and their effect on one another.

4 Oil is a liquid, steam is a gas, and copper is a solid.

5 People breathe in oxygen and breathe out carbon dioxide. Cars give off carbon monoxide.

6 Scientists working in laboratories often use glass test tubes to carry out experiments.

7 An atom is the smallest unit that an element can be divided into, and a cell is the smallest unit of a plant or animal.

8 The discovery of electricity, which led to the invention of the light bulb, was a huge breakthrough in scientific knowledge.

Answers

1 living   2 substances   3 energy   4 liquid, gas, solid
5 oxygen, carbon dioxide, carbon monoxide   6 laboratories, test tubes, experiments   7 atom, element, cell   8 discovery, invention, breakthrough

3 Ask the class the question and elicit some examples. Perhaps also ask what kind of projects or experiments students have taken part in at school or college.

Part 2

4 After the class have studied the Quick steps, elicit the pronunciation of the numbers, then ask for more examples of those students find difficult. Make sure that students can spell the written forms: these must be correct in Part 2 if they choose to write them out rather than use the numerals. Also draw attention to any conventions that may differ from those in students' first language, e.g. using a comma for decimal places, or a full stop to denote thousands.

Answers

thirty-first, nineteen eighty-nine, four hundred and sixty-three, three point five five, twelfth, sixty per cent, one/a third, twelve thousand three hundred, thirty-five degrees, twenty-second, twenty fifteen *or* two thousand and fifteen, three-quarters

5 Give students a minute to look at the questions and either mark the questions that require numbers, or note them down. Go through the answers, but without giving away too much information.

Answers

1 age   2 year   5 fraction/percentage   6 number   10 date

6 ◯ *2.09* Look at the Exam tips with the class, then tell students to work on their own. Play the recording through twice without pausing.

Recording script

You will hear a journalist reporting on a prize for young scientists and engineers. For questions 1–10, complete the sentences.

Ryan

The National Science and Engineering Competition is aimed at young scientists and engineers who have developed new ideas completely of their own. They may be school projects or something they've done as a hobby, and the winners are awarded prizes and named Young Scientist and Young Engineer of the Year. Anyone aged 18 or under can take part, although (1) <u>the science category was won by a 17-year-old last year, as was the engineering one</u>. The competition covers every area of science, technology, engineering and mathematics, and is intentionally broadly based so as to encourage as many young people as possible to enter.

It's been going for a few years now. In fact, (2) <u>it's been an annual event since 2009</u>, although it became much bigger in 2010 once more people became aware of it. And then the media started to take an interest in the Big Bang Fair, where the winners are announced. From that year on, there have been lectures by top speakers, and shows put on by national television channels.

The Big Bang Fair is a three-day fair for school students interested in science and engineering, with lots of things to do like interactive science quizzes, games and activities. For instance, one boy had set up a non-moving bicycle, like those you find in a gym, and was pedalling away energetically. But (3) <u>this was about electricity</u> rather than exercise, with a challenge to anyone present to generate more than he could, as measured by the attached equipment. Nobody managed to, at least while I was around.

So they have a good time there, with plenty of fun things to do. But its real purpose is more serious: (4) <u>to promote careers in those subjects</u>, especially where there is a national skills gap in particular areas. This is done in a wide range of ways, and a study into how this can be extended is currently being carried out by the Centre for Science Education.

The fair is becoming increasingly popular. The total number of people at the most recent one was over 22,500, of whom (5) <u>at least two-thirds, according to the figures I have, would have been of secondary-school age</u>, with teachers and parents making up rather less than a quarter between them. Over 110 public and private organisations from across the country were represented, and it was clear that everyone there had a genuine desire to raise awareness of young people's achievements in science and technology.

Naturally, the number of young people actually involved in the competition was smaller. They can enter either as individuals or as part of a team, so that whereas in total 193 projects were presented, (6) <u>there were actually 312 competitors</u> working in the fields of science, technology, mathematics and engineering.

And there were some great projects. In one I particularly liked, the team built quite complicated structures in the shape of road bridges … entirely in chocolate. Most were surprisingly strong, though of course any that collapsed could simply be eaten. In another, a team managed to (7) <u>convert coffee into a gas that then became the source of energy for a car, successfully</u>

covering the 300 kilometres to the fair. Finding alternatives to petrol as a fuel was a common theme, not surprisingly, with many entries aimed at reducing the amount of carbon monoxide and carbon dioxide being released into the atmosphere.

The final is held at the Big Bang Fair, where the number of entries is reduced to a shortlist of six. Neither individuals nor teams need to make a formal presentation to a big audience, but they are expected to be able to give a clear (8) explanation, going into some detail about their project so that it can be properly assessed by the five judges.

They may well be asked things about it, too, partly to see how well they respond to questions. Although the quality of the work they do is the main thing, (9) their communication skills are also taken into account as the winners may have the chance to speak in public, including on TV, on behalf of young scientists and engineers. And that, not surprisingly, appeals to quite a lot of teenagers.

Everyone's keen to know who's won this year, but it's quite a long process and although all entries had to be in by October the thirty-first, we'll have to wait until nearly the spring to find out. It'll actually be (10) on the first day of the next Big Bang Fair, which runs from March the eleventh to the thirteenth. I'm sure that will be followed with a lot of interest.

Exam task answers

1 17   2 2009   3 electricity   4 careers   5 two-thirds / $^2/_3$
6 312   7 coffee   8 explanation   9 communication skills
10 March (the) eleventh / March 11th / March 11 *or* the eleventh of March / 11th March / 11 March

Optional activity

You may want to play the recording again to highlight some of the distraction used, e.g. in question 3 *this was about electricity rather than exercise* has two uncountable nouns very close together.

Grammar

Review of passive forms

1 This activity can be done in pairs. Begin by eliciting the reasons why we use the passive, i.e. when we don't know or don't need to say who or what did something, when what happens is more important than who did it, and in formal styles – including processes in science and technology. Get students to underline the passive verbs in the extracts, and check the answers. Go through the answers with the class, ensuring that everyone is clear what a past participle is. With some classes you could compare the extensive use of the passive in English with equivalent forms in students' first language(s). In some cases reflexive verbs may be used instead of the passive. For an example of the passive with *get*, and of the separation of the auxiliary from *be*, refer a strong class back to the Reading text: *all the news stories that won't get written, or the songs that will never be recorded*. Explain that *get* is only used when something changes or happens, especially to somebody or something.

Answers

is done, can be extended, is (currently) being carried out
1 be   2 past participle (of the main verb)

2 Tell students to change the verbs from active to passive and then do the matching activity. Focus on 4 and elicit the use of the preposition *by* plus a noun if we want to say who or what did the action. Also point out that the passive tends to be used in more formal styles, including news reports, letters, and processes in science and technology. Elicit the two possible forms in 5. See also Exercise 3 below.

Answers

1 The equipment has been broken.
2 Firstly, the liquid is heated up.
3 Safety glasses must be worn in the laboratory.
4 This year's Science Competition was won by a very young student.
5 Dr Liu is said to be a brilliant scientist. / It is said that Dr Liu is a brilliant scientist.
1 b   2 a   3 d   4 e   5 c

3 Get students to correct the mistakes, then go through the answers, accepting alternatives. Tell them to be careful with 6 – they need to understand *at school* (see Articles in Speaking in this unit). Then focus attention on 5 and 8. Explain that these forms are often used when we don't know, or aren't interested in, who *says*, *thinks*, *feels*, *suggests* (etc.) something, and are frequently used in formal texts and news reports. Encourage students to use them in exam Writing tasks such as essays, articles, reports and reviews. Highlight the impersonal *it* in 5 and the perfect infinitive in 8. Elicit more examples of these forms, using human interest stories in the news, e.g. *They are believed to be getting divorced*, and highlight the passive infinitive form, e.g. *a suspect is said to have been arrested*.

Answers

1 was invented   2 is being made   3 will be asked   4 painted
5 *correct*   6 used to be taught   7 had been born   8 *correct*

4 Tell the class to begin by quickly gist-reading the text. Answer any vocabulary questions that students may have, e.g. *absorb*, *radio waves*, *convert*, *appliance*, then get them to write down their answers. Go through the answers, highlighting those cases where the passive is far more likely than the active, e.g. items 6, 8 and 10. Also focus on the position of *already* in item 9 – this may be tested in Reading and Use of English Part 4.

Answers

1 a meal is warmed up   2 radio waves are absorbed by the food
3 the meal is being cooked   4 the food has been heated up
5 the radio waves will not have been absorbed by these materials
6 microwaving can be described   7 the microwave is often thought of   8 it was invented   9 they were already being used by restaurants   10 over a million had been sold

5 Divide the class into pairs. You may want to prompt pairs with suitable verbs, but without giving the game away. Monitor students for accuracy in their use of passive forms, and encourage a variety of tenses. If time allows, get students to choose a second or third appliance, and repeat the activity.

6 Students complete the sentences, if necessary referring to the Grammar reference. Check their answers for accuracy, pointing out that these forms may be tested in Reading and Use of English Part 4, and elsewhere.

> **Answers**
> 2 is believed that there is water on that distant planet
> 3 are known to be dangerous
> 4 are thought to have made a breakthrough
> 5 is considered essential to have a mobile phone
> 6 is reported that doctors have found a cure

7 Encourage pairs to discuss any reports they have heard or read including – but not only – science and technology issues. If necessary, give short prompts such as *doctors found a cure*, *a new kind of computer* or *a new species*. Elicit some of the points, and ask the rest of the class if they have heard the same reports, and whether they are believable.

Speaking
Articles

1 This activity can be done in pairs. Elicit the terms *definite article* for *the* and *indefinite article* for *a/an*, and point out that their uses may in some cases be different from those in students' first language (if indeed they have articles at all). Many of the mistakes in Exercise 2 can be attributed to this. If students find the task at all difficult, prompt with some examples, e.g. *When we mention it for the first time, do we say 'I've got new bike', 'I've got the new bike' or 'I've got a new bike'?* Then go through the answers, eliciting examples of each rule and reference, e.g. *she is a chemist*, *a thousand*.

> **Answers**
> 1 a/an   2 the   3 no article

2 Give students plenty of time to correct the mistakes. You may or may not want to point out that there is only one mistake in each sentence – the correct use of articles with other nouns makes the task more challenging. Go through the answers, eliciting the reason in each case.

> **Answers**
> 1 from flu (illness)   2 the telephone (invention)
> 3 the army (only one)   4 the greatest (superlative)
> 5 a 7.8 per cent (number)   6 the piano (musical instrument)
> 7 an engineer (job)   8 a very interesting job (first time mentioned)

3 🔘 *2.10* Point out that these two students are practising Speaking Part 3, and that Part 4 follows on from this with the same speakers. Give students time to fill in or note down their answers, then play the recording once or twice, highlighting the /ə/ in *the* and *a*.

> **Recording script**
>
> Lena: I think geology would be the most interesting science to study. It's a pity we don't do it at school because I like the idea of becoming a geologist.
>
> Felix: I think the one that appeals to me most is zoology. It'd be fantastic to get a job in the countryside in Africa studying animals like the lion or leopard.

> **Answers**
> 1 –   2 the   3 a   4 –   5 the   6 a   7 the   8 –   9 a   10 the   11 –   12 –   13 the

Part 4

4 🔘 *2.11* Explain that students will hear an extract from Part 4. Play the recording once, and get them to note down the numbers. Check the answers, then play the recording again so that students can tick the phrases used, or write them down (in this case pausing if necessary). Then go through the answers.

> **Recording script**
>
> Teacher: Lena, how important is it that people study science?
>
> Lena: It's quite important, I think, because the country will need a lot of scientists in the future. <u>As well as that</u>, people need to understand science so they can make the right choices when they buy things. <u>And not only that</u>, they can also make better decisions on how to protect the environment.
>
> Felix: Yes, I agree. <u>And there's another thing</u>: they can make more sense of the world around them, learning things like how electricity works and which chemicals are dangerous, and that can make people safer. <u>And also</u> how the human body works, which can help them lead healthier lives.

> **Answers**
> Lena 3, Felix 2; as well as that, and not only that, and there's another thing, and also

5 Pairs choose the *Do* or *Did* form of the question depending on whether they are still at school, and still doing science there. Monitor their speaking.

6 Tell groups only to note down the points, as in Exercise 5, not to discuss them at this stage.

7 Students stay in the same groups as for Exercise 6. Tell the 'examiners' to ask the same three or four questions to each 'candidate', unless the candidates themselves ask each other to comment. Time the groups so that they speak for no more than four minutes. You may want to suggest that groups record the dialogue on their mobile phones, for instance, and then play back the recording. Get them to comment on each other's use of passives and articles. Encourage examiners to say how well candidates did. Stress the importance of being polite and constructive in any criticism, and giving equal measures of praise.

Reading and Use of English

Collocations

1 Pairs or students working on their own could be allowed to use dictionaries for the matching task, although the IT words will probably be familiar to those who use English-language software. Check the answers.

> **Answers**
>
> attach a file, browse websites, carry out an experiment, charge a mobile phone, prove a theory, run a program, store data, undo a change

2 Allow the use of dictionaries. There are some useful B2-level words here. Go through the answers, the collocates and the distractors.

> **Answers**
>
> 1 A (voice)   2 D (computer)   3 A (screen)   4 B (PC)
> 5 C (two numbers)   6 C (of two things)   7 D (computer)

Part 1

3 Directly elicit some answers, or get pairs or small groups to discuss them first. Allow a minute or two for this gist-reading activity, then elicit brief answers.

> **Answers**
>
> in the text: tell people where they are, helping in emergencies/accidents, search and rescue, weather forecasting, seeing into space, phone calls, the Internet, TV
> also: mapping the ground, searching for archaeological sites, pollution monitoring

4 Give students a few minutes to find the collocations. Point out that more than one word may collocate, and it is not always next to the missing word. You may want to go through the answers now, which might make the exam task a little easier, or wait until the class have completed the exam task. Give students only 10–12 minutes for the gap-filling task, bearing in mind that they have already read the text and identified at least some collocations.

> **Answers**
>
> 1 positioning (systems)   2 emergency   3 space   4 space
> 5 ten, more clearly than   6 phone calls   7 the Internet
> 8 TV programmes
>
> **Exam task answers**
>
> 1 A   2 B   3 A   4 A   5 B   6 D   7 C   8 D

5 Allow only a minute for this, then elicit the answers. Many of the options are B2-level vocabulary items which you may want to focus on.

Writing

Reason and result links

1 Students could do this activity in pairs. They should already know basic linkers such as *because* and *so*, but these are quite simple and learning the expressions presented here will enable them to vary the language they use in their writing. Give students some time to complete the expressions, which they should be able to do without using dictionaries. Go through the answers, eliciting more example sentences if time allows.

> **Answers**
>
> 1 result   2 why   3 owing   4 account   5 Consequently/Therefore   6 reason   7 Since/Because   8 view
> 9 because   10 consequently/therefore
> *Quite formal:* owing to, on account of, consequently, in view of the fact that, therefore

Part 2 article

2 Allow just 30 seconds for the class to think about the questions, then elicit the answers.

> **Answers**
>
> 1 readers of an international magazine
> 2 you may win a prize
> 3 give reasons why the most important piece of technology you have is so important to you, say how it could be improved

3 Give students plenty of time to answer the questions, then go through the answers with the class.

> **Suggested answers**
>
> 1 neutral: it uses contracted forms, e.g. *couldn't*, and one informal word (*lappy*), but is not generally conversational in tone. It is written in complete sentences, some of them fairly complex, and uses passive forms. It uses full reason and result links, but not the more formal ones.
> 2 good things: first and second; problems and improvements: third and fourth
> 3 a title that catches the eye, expressing enthusiasm for the subject; the possibility of linking the mind directly to the laptop, and what that could lead to

4 In item a, point out that some links differ slightly from those in the exercise above, and that students should try to use these variants, too. Answer any other language questions students may have about meaning, e.g. *mains electricity*, *touchpad*. You may also want to point out how the article aims to keep the reader interested by varying the types of sentence, using shorter and more complex sentences, as well as both coordination and subordination.

> **Answers**
>
> a since, As a result, because of, that is why, for that reason
> b I couldn't imagine a world without laptops, Without my lappy, my life would crash
> c they can't always be connected, batteries are needed

5 Refer the class to the Quick steps, then get them to brainstorm ideas for their own articles. It's probably best not to elicit answers.

6 Allow just 35–40 minutes for writing as students have already studied the task. Remind them to leave at least five minutes of that for checking, which could be done as a peer correction activity.

Model answer

Cool technology

It was invented half a century ago, though it hasn't changed much since then. We all seem to have one because it makes life so much easier, yet we hardly notice it's there. So what is it?

It's the freezer, that unexciting-looking box in the kitchen that keeps the fridge company. But whereas food in the fridge only stays fresh for a few days, the freezer allows it to be kept for weeks or even months.

Consequently, food can be bought in large amounts, saving both time and money. As well as that, any food left over from meals can be stored for another day, rather than having to be thrown out.

My favourite use of my freezer is for frozen fruit and vegetables. These, believe it or not, are particularly good for you, as they are frozen just when they are ripe. Fresh fruit and vegetables, in contrast, are often picked too early.

The only improvement I would make to my freezer is to make it bigger, so I can keep even more icecream in it!

Revision

1 Answers

Across
1 cell   3 backup   4 undo   6 run   7 global   9 data   12 update
14 browse   15 crash
Down
1 charge   2 launch   3 blog   5 faint   8 outer   10 access
11 atom   13 prove   14 bug

2 Answers

1 times   2 charge   3 outer   4 access   5 video   6 exploration

3 Answers

1 the   2 a   3 –   4 –   5 the   6 the   7 an   8 a   9 the   10 a
11 the   12 the   13 –   14 the   15 –   16 the   17 –   18 –
19 a   20 the

4 Answers

1 might not | have been   2 are expected | to fall suddenly
3 it is | even suggested (that)   4 is believed that | carelessness was
5 is said | to have been   6 are being | changed constantly / constantly changed

Remind students that there is more practice on the CD-ROM.

9 Fame and the media

Unit objectives

TOPICS	the media, celebrities
GRAMMAR	review of reported speech and reporting verbs
VOCABULARY	media vocabulary, noun suffixes
READING and USE OF ENGLISH	Part 7: focusing on key words
	Part 3: noun suffixes, internal spelling changes
WRITING	Part 2 report: recommending
LISTENING	Part 4: predicting content
SPEAKING	Part 2: keeping going

Listening

Media vocabulary

1 This activity could be done in pairs. Some of these mainly B2-level expressions may be new to the class, so let students use dictionaries where necessary. Then elicit the answers plus the meaning of each word and phrase.

> **Answers**
>
> *television and radio*: broadcasting, commercials, episode, network, remote control, satellite dish
> *newspapers and magazines*: circulation, gossip column, illustrations, print version, publication, tabloids, the press
> *both*: news items, the headlines

2 Elicit a list of kinds of TV programmes. Make sure the class list includes those listed below. Either let students briefly discuss their viewing habits in pairs and then answer any questions about language that they may have, or else elicit the answers directly from the class. With a monolingual class, elicit some examples from TV in their country. With a multilingual class, ask about talent/reality/quiz programmes shown in many countries, e.g. *The X Factor*.

> **Suggested answers**
>
> comedies, current affairs programmes, drama series, documentaries, live sports, news bulletins, quiz shows, soap operas, talent shows

3 Give students a little time to discuss the vocabulary, using their dictionaries if necessary, and briefly say why they would prefer one of these TV jobs. Go through the meanings with the class, and elicit a few reasons for choosing particular jobs. Focus particularly on *presenter*, as this will be the topic of the Listening text.

> **Answers**
>
> camera operator: person who films a programme (*also* 'cameraman' or 'camerawoman')
> editor: person who corrects or changes parts of a programme before it is shown
> interviewer: person who asks the questions during TV interviews, especially with celebrities
> investigative journalist: reporter who tries to discover hidden information of public interest
> newsreader: person who reads out the news in a news bulletin (*also* newscaster, especially US English)
> news reporter: person who obtains information about news events and describes them for TV
> presenter: person who introduces a TV show
> producer: person who controls how a programme is made
> scriptwriter: person who writes the words for programmes
> set designer: person who is responsible for the visual aspects of a programme

Part 4

4 Give the class a few seconds to read the instructions, then elicit the answers.

> **Answers**
>
> 1 an interview   2 Kirsty Ross, a television presenter
> 3 her work

5 ⊙ 2.12 Allow a minute for students working on their own to note down the kind of information they need to listen for. You may want to go through the answers now, or – to avoid making the exam task any easier – leave it until students have completed Exercise 6. Play the recording twice, without pausing.

> **Answers**
>
> 1 occupation *or* what   2 activity *or* how   3 opinion
> 4 activity *or* how   5 feelings   6 attitude   7 opinion

> **Recording script**
>
> *You will hear part of a radio interview with Kirsty Ross, who works as a television presenter. For questions 1–7, choose the best answer (A, B or C).*
>
> Interviewer: Now I have a guest whose voice will be familiar to many listeners: TV presenter Kirsty Ross. Good morning Kirsty, and welcome to radio!
>
> Kirsty: Good morning!
>
> Interviewer: To start off, why did you choose presenting as a career? Had you done media studies or something like that at university?
>
> Kirsty: Actually (1) I'd been working in entertainment ever since I left school. I was the keyboard player in a band. I was having loads of fun but it wasn't leading anywhere and what really fascinated me was television. I'd thought of trying acting and getting into TV that way, but I think I felt I wanted to be myself in front of the camera, and that's why I decided on presenting.

Interviewer: And how did you manage to get into it? There must be thousands of people out there with the same ambition.

Kirsty: Yes, I knew there would be a lot of competition for the few jobs going, and that just watching TV all day long and trying to imitate those doing the presenting wouldn't bring success. I looked at specialist courses for would-be presenters but they were all too expensive, so instead (2) <u>I spent six months doing work experience. It was a difficult time because of course I wasn't earning anything, but being right inside a major TV organisation taught me a lot.</u>

Interviewer: What did you do after that finished?

Kirsty: I made a short film of myself, about three minutes long, showing off what I felt to be my strongest points.

Interviewer: What are they?

Kirsty: People say I'm good at looking straight into the camera and talking, and I've always enjoyed getting into conversation with a live audience, but (3) <u>being able to ask guests the right questions and get good answers out of them is what I take most pride in.</u> Though I'm probably awful as an interviewee – sitting here being asked all these questions is making me nervous! Anyway, in those days people used to record their own films on video and post them to the production company.

Interviewer: Did you do that?

Kirsty: I was going to, but then I had this sudden fear about mail getting lost and it was so important to me that (4) <u>I took it round to their office myself.</u> Of course, if I were starting out these days I'd send it electronically as an attachment as everyone does now.

Interviewer: And how did they respond?

Kirsty: They asked me if I would go in for a test the next week.

Interviewer: That must have been good news for you.

Kirsty: Yes, you'd have thought I'd be delighted, wouldn't you? Though actually I'd been hoping that once they'd seen my film I'd be offered a job straightaway, so (5) <u>when I heard I'd have to go there and perform live in front of the bosses, I began to worry about what might go wrong.</u> At the same time, though, I knew I could rise to the challenge.

Interviewer: Which I imagine you did.

Kirsty: It went quite well, yes. Though they made it clear I had a lot to learn before they'd actually put me in front of live TV cameras.

Interviewer: What kind of things?

Kirsty: Well, they said I'd need to practise memorising scripts, but of course I'd spent years learning music and lyrics off by heart so I was used to that kind of thing. (6) <u>What was trickier was knowing where you're supposed to be looking at any given point when you have cameras either side of you and right in front.</u> Fortunately you get some guidance from the producer, who's in touch with you through the earpiece, a small listening device that fits in your ear, so she can give you precise instructions while you're going out live.

Interviewer: And what would you say a presenter most needs to be able to do?

Kirsty: Well it helps a lot if you have a good working relationship with the others in the studio: the producer, the camera operators, the make-up people – everybody, in fact. And on the other hand it's good if you can work on your own, Googling the people you're going to interview, for instance, and the topics you'll be talking about. But (7) <u>none of this matters unless you and everybody around you knows that whatever happens you won't panic. They have to be able to trust you to carry on as normal,</u> even if something truly awful occurs.

Interviewer: Has anything ever gone badly wrong while you were presenting live?

Kirsty: Yes, it's happened recently. Last week my guest suddenly walked out because ...

Exam task answers

1 C   2 C   3 A   4 A   5 B   6 B   7 A

6 Give everyone a few seconds to check they haven't missed any out, then go through the answers. You may want to point out that multiple-choice questions sometimes rely on understanding superlatives for the correct answer, e.g. the speaker might say several qualities are important but only one of these will be the most important.

Grammar

Review of reported speech and reporting verbs

1 This activity could be done in pairs. Give students plenty of time to study the sentences, then check the answers.

Answers

a I have a guest whose voice will be familiar.
b Sitting here being asked all these questions is making me nervous.
c It's happened recently. Last week my guest suddenly walked out.

2 Elicit the changes, or non-changes, to other forms, e.g. modals: most remain the same, although *can* becomes *could*, *may* changes to *might* in the past, and *must* (though not *mustn't*) usually changes to *had to*.

Answers

present simple → past simple, *will* future → conditional, present continuous → past continuous, present perfect → past perfect, past simple → past perfect

3 Check students' answers and elicit as many other expressions that change as possible. Ask for an example sentence in each case.

Answers

I → he, here → there, these → those, me → her, last week → the week before, my → her
demonstratives: this → that; personal pronouns I → she, we/ you → they; possessive adjectives: our/your → their, my → his; reflexive pronouns: myself → herself, etc.; time expressions: today → the previous day, next week → the following week, etc.

4 Tell the class to write their answers, then go through these, checking particularly for correct word order.

Answers

1 Jaime said he didn't want to watch that programme then *or* at that time.
2 Louise told me over the phone she was going out when her boyfriend got there.
3 On Monday Joey said he'd / he had seen the match at his friend's house the night before *or* the previous night.
4 My sister said (that) later that evening she'd / she would be talking to her favourite TV star.
5 Anna told the presenter (that) she'd been working in entertainment ever since she left school. (tense stays the same)
6 Julia said she'd / she had always wanted to be on TV, and the day after *or* the next day *or* the following day she would be.

5 Allow a minute for students to change the questions, then elicit them. Then allow a couple of minutes to work out the rules before they refer to the Grammar reference. Go through the answers, pointing out that mistakes by exam candidates with reported questions are very common, particularly the use of direct question word order and the use of *do/did*. Also remind them that questions marks are not used in these forms.

Answers

a if/whether she had done / she'd done that
b how they had / they'd responded
To make questions: we use the same word order as in a statement, without *do* or *did*, making the same tense etc.

6 Make sure that everyone understands that *to* refers to a full infinitive, *-ing* to the present participle, and so on. Give students a few minutes to complete the sentences, then check the answers. Elicit more examples with each verb.

Answers

2 suggested   3 told   4 apologised   5 admitted

7 Students put the remaining four verbs from Exercise 6 into the correct group. They then do the same for the verbs in Exercise 7. Suggest students imagine sentences containing each verb to help them. If they get stuck on any, let them use their dictionaries to check. Go through the answers, eliciting at least one example sentence for each reporting verb.

Answers

a *to*: decide, promise, refuse, threaten
b object + *to*: advise, invite, order, persuade, remind, tell, warn
c *-ing*: admit, deny, recommend, suggest
d (*that*) + clause: decide, deny, explain, promise, recommend, tell, threaten, warn
e preposition + *-ing*: advise (against), apologise (for), insist (on)

8 Students complete the sentences, which all require reporting-verb structures, individually. Go through the answers with the class, pointing out how marks are allocated.

Answers

1 refused to listen | to me   2 reminded us | to bring our
3 invited Jo to meet | her
4 denied doing *or* denied having done | anything wrong
5 advised her | against going
6 suggested going *or* suggested we go | that way

Optional activity

Dictate the following sentence starters for students to complete.

1 The interviewers asked me to
2 My parents said that
3 I persuaded my friend
4 My friend asked me whether
5 One of the players had to apologise
6 I promised my friend
7 A lifeguard warned people on the beach not
8 My teacher recommended that I

You may want to check students' written sentences, or elicit answers from volunteers.

Suggested answers

1 answer some questions.
2 I had to come home early.
3 to go camping with me. *or* that we should go camping.
4 I had seen that TV show the night before.
5 for saying something rude to the referee.
6 that I would help her.
7 to go into the sea.
8 should aim for a career in the media.

Reading and Use of English
Part 7

1 Students can discuss the questions in pairs or small groups, or the discussion could be done as a brief class activity.

2 Give students a minute to note down their answers, then check.

Answers

1 people who have become famous in their country
2 four people   3 celebrities for different reasons

3 Focus attention on the Quick steps, then get students to underline the key words in pencil, or write these down in their notebooks. Don't go through the answers yet. Then give the class about 20 minutes to do the multiple-matching task, in exam conditions.

Suggested key-word answers

1 expensive   2 regrets   3 media, aggressive   4 set an example
5 advise   6 most, enjoy   7 impossible, secret, media
8 more important   9 suspicious, other celebrities
10 wishes, hadn't said

Exam task answers

1 A   2 D   3 B   4 C   5 A   6 D   7 D   8 C   9 B   10 C

4 Allow 30 seconds for students to make sure that they have answered all the questions, reminding them that in the exam they will have to leave enough time to complete the answer sheet. Go through the answers, and also ask the class which key words they underlined in Exercise 3.

5 Encourage the use of a variety of reporting verbs where possible. With a strong class, this exercise could be done orally. Otherwise, give the class a few minutes to write down their answers, then check.

Answers

(note: *that* is possible after the reporting verbs)
2 Jake said he was meeting some big stars, and he was doing worthwhile things, too.
3 Jake said he had to leave extra-large tips in case they recognised him. *or* Jake complained ...
4 Rachita said she had made good friends on that show.
5 Rachita said she was happy as she was.
6 Elka said winning that gold medal had changed her life.
7 Marcos said it was a pity he hadn't / had not realised sooner. *or* Marcos admitted ...
8 Marcos said that the press would always find out every personal detail. *or* Marcos complained ...

6 Point out that the letters in brackets refer to the sections. Give students a few minutes to find these B2-level expressions, then go through the answers.

Answers

1 guest   2 agent   3 film rights   4 being in the public eye
5 microphones   6 show off   7 look down on   8 inspire
9 role model   10 publicity   11 privacy
12 making a name for themselves

7 Give students, working in pairs or small groups, a few minutes to discuss being famous as a chat show guest, TV actor, sports star and singer, then ask the class what they felt about being famous for each of these reasons. Encourage the use of vocabulary from Exercise 6.

Speaking

Keeping going

1 🔘 *2.13* Explain that students are going to hear a strong student discussing the two photos for about a minute. Allow a little time for students to look at the photos and points

1–8, and tell them to tick these if and when they hear them mentioned, though the speaker won't use these exact words. Play the recording once or twice, then check the answers.

Answer

all except 7

Recording script

Well, both are about the media, but one of them is taking place in a studio and the other outdoors. There are two people in the studio and they are sitting while those in the street are standing, and <u>another difference is</u> that the TV presenter has some notes to refer to whereas the reporters are simply listening as the woman gives an explanation of what happened. She has a sad expression on her face and the reporters look quite serious too, but in the studio both the people there are smiling and seem relaxed. Of course, that interview is for entertainment and the other one is for a news story. <u>There's also the fact that</u> their appearance is different, not just because those in the studio are younger, also because they're wearing indoor clothes. <u>As well as that</u>, there are some other people in the street though they aren't taking any notice of them, but in the studio there's probably an audience who are enjoying the interview.

2 🔘 *2.13* Play the recording again, then check the answers. Remind the class that this is about the amount of time they will need to speak for in Speaking Part 2, so a lot of points can be covered.

Answers

another difference is, There's also the fact that, As well as that

3 Put students into groups that don't contain their usual partners. Remind the class that Maruja mentioned seven points of similarity and difference between her two situations. Set up this activity as a competition: Which group can come up with the most points? Give any further details that students may want for the situations, then let them do the activity, making brief notes for each point. When they have finished, ask each group how many points they have, and get them to give you some examples, but don't do this as a class discussion.

Suggested answers

both probably for TV, both show cameras and camera operators, both show people concentrating on their work, both programmes probably being recorded, probably hot in both situations, TV crew have to keep quiet in both situations, outdoors *and* in studio, three people *and* a lot of people, crew sitting and hiding *and* crew standing and clearly visible, dressed for outdoor heat in shorts, etc. *and* dressed for urban indoors, subjects are animals *and* subjects are actors, unaware they are being filmed *and* aware they are being filmed, potentially dangerous situation *and* safe situation

4 Make sure that both students in each pair were not together in Exercise 3, and get them to take turns speaking while their partner times them using a watch or mobile phone stopwatch. When they have finished, ask them how they got on. If time allows, elicit the points the class mentioned for the situations.

Part 2

5 Tell pairs to look at the instructions, not the photos. Give them a minute, then check the answers.

6 Draw students' attention to the Quick steps before they plan what to include when they speak. Get pairs to time each other as they do the task. Monitor them, ensuring that the non-speaker does not interrupt until the minute is up.

7 Pairs then change roles and repeat the task.

8 You may also want students to comment on the number of points their partners mention. If so, remind them to be diplomatic and constructive.

Reading and Use of English

Noun suffixes

1 This activity could be done in pairs. Give students two or three minutes to answer the questions, then elicit the answers. You may want to put the verb forms on the board so that the class can compare the verbs and the nouns.

Answers

a appear + -ance   b explain + -ation (explain *drops* i)
c entertain + -ment   d express + -ion   e differ + -ence

2 Point out that other spelling changes from those in Exercise 1 will be needed in some cases. You might want to tell students what these may be, e.g. *y* changes to *i*, drops *e*, adds *t*. Allow plenty of time for students to write the verbs in the correct groups. If they are stuck on any particular words, give these orally to see if they can work out the correct spelling. Go through all the answers, checking for correct spelling in each case. Remind the class that any of these words (the nouns are all B2 level) could be tested in Reading and Use of English Part 3, or elsewhere in the exam.

Answers

-ance: disappearance, maintenance (ai *changes to* e)
-ation: expectation, identification (y *changes to* i, *adds* c), recommendation, variation (y *changes to* i)
-ment: arrangement, requirement
-ion: contribution (*drops* e), intention (d *changes to* t), introduction (*drops* e, *adds* t)
-ence: existence, preference

3 Point out that all these mistakes focus on the five noun suffixes students have practised. When students have worked through these, check their answers and spelling. Elicit the verbs that the nouns are formed from.

Answers

1 explanation (explain)   2 advertisement (advertise)
3 suggestions (suggest)   4 requirements (require)
5 reduction (reduce)   6 solutions (solve)

Part 3

4 Explain that in Part 3 students will need to change the internal spelling of some words, e.g. *explain – explanation*. Practise the pronunciation of the words that may cause difficulties, e.g. *height*, *depth*. Focus attention on the example and make sure that everyone knows what they have to do. When students have finished, go through the answers, eliciting the spelling of each base word. Point out that these changes are sometimes tested in Reading and Use of English Part 3.

Answers

2 choice, choose   3 height, high   4 proof, prove   5 depth, deep

5 Give the class no more than a minute to skim the text and answer the gist-question. Elicit the answer, then get students to work on their own for ten minutes on the exam task, either filling in or noting down their answers.

Answer

No, he does not believe it has reached its peak.

Exam task answers

1 publication   2 organisation   3 length   4 advertisements/adverts   5 variety   6 viewers   7 choice   8 belief

6 Give everyone a minute or so to read through the completed text and to check their spelling, then go through the answers. Ask students to spell out the answers. You may also want to focus on the suffixes added, and the reasons why items 4 and 6 require plural nouns.

Optional activity

Ask if students think young people are watching more or less television these days. They could discuss the question in pairs or as a class. Encourage the use of language from the text such as *rate of increase* and *long-term trend*, which may be useful when students write reports of their own in Writing on the next page.

Writing

Part 2 report

1 Students could do this activity in pairs. Give them a few minutes to complete the expressions, and be ready to help out with language questions, particularly the useful B2-level language used in this exercise, such as *recommendation*, *step*, *survey*, *approved of* and *key* (adjective). Go through the answers with the class, and suggest that they use some of these expressions whenever they write reports.

Answers

1 recommendation   2 conclusion   3 step   4 sum
5 challenge   6 carried out   7 purpose

Optional activity

Give students time to work out which expressions from Exercise 1 can be used in which part of a report: the introduction, the findings, the end. Elicit the answers.

Answers

introduction: purpose; findings: challenge, carried out; end: recommendation, conclusion, step, sum

2 Give the class 30 seconds to think about the questions, then elicit the answers.

Answers

1 a group of English-speaking people
2 they are planning to visit your town next winter
3 information about the television and radio there
4 which kinds of programme you think the group might enjoy watching and listening to

3 Give students plenty of time to answer the questions, then go through the answers.

Answers

1 five
2 yes
3 neutral or fairly formal
4 the sports, nature and arts programmes on TV, films and drama series in English with subtitles, 24-hour music radio stations
5 a The aim of this report is to, I strongly recommend, To sum up
   b In addition, also, while, too, and, To sum up, even if
   c Many tourists have said they were able to enjoy ...

4 Refer the class to the Quick steps, then get them to brainstorm ideas on their own. It is probably best not to elicit answers.

5 Allow 35 – 40 minutes for writing as students have already studied the task. Remind them to leave at least five minutes for checking, which could be done as peer correction.

Model answer

The local media
The purpose of this report is to provide information about the broadcast media in this town, and to make recommendations for visitors.

Radio
The main national stations are: Radio 1, which broadcasts news and discussion programmes; Radio 2, offering pop music and lifestyle features; and Radio 3, which mainly plays classical music. In addition, there are several local stations. These provide coverage of news stories from the area, chat about topical issues, and regular phone-ins.

Television
As with radio, there are both local and national broadcasts, while the main international channels are available in most homes and hotels via cable or satellite TV. There are also several channels that show the latest films, although these normally require payment.

Recommendations
Visitors will find local radio and TV stations of particular interest for traffic updates, weather forecasts and details of what's on in sport and culture. For music and live sports coverage, national radio is highly recommended. For the latest news, both TV1 and TV2 broadcast regular bulletins covering national and international events, accompanied by well-informed discussion and analysis.

Revision

1 Answers

1 talent show   2 satellite dish   3 gossip column
4 investigative journalist   5 drama series   6 camera operator
The unused compound nouns are *current affairs*, *remote control*, *set designer* and *soap opera*.

2 Answers

1 he looked   2 he was   3 was wrong   4 (that) he had / he'd lost his job the previous   5 if/whether he had / he'd told his
6 he couldn't   7 her (that) his dad was in prison   8 his mum was   9 (that) she had / she'd disappeared the week   10 him what he would do   11 (that) he didn't know   12 (that) he was thinking

3 Answers

1 promised to talk | to her   2 warned us | not to touch
3 how deep | the river was   4 apologised for | interrupting my
5 asked (her) whether/if | she knew
6 their hands where | he could

4 Answers

1 readers   2 illustrations   3 depth   4 entertainment
5 humorous   6 recommendations   7 powerful   8 editors

> Remind students that there is more practice on the CD-ROM.

10 Clothing and shopping

Unit objectives

TOPICS	shopping and consumer goods, fashion
GRAMMAR	position of adverbs of manner and opinion, review of *wish* and *if only*, review of causative *have* and *get*
VOCABULARY	clothing and shopping vocabulary, phrasal verbs with *out*, extreme adjectives
READING and	Part 6: development of ideas, linking expressions, position of adverbs
USE OF ENGLISH	Part 4: focus on individual items
WRITING	Part 1 essay: extreme adjectives
LISTENING	Part 3: focusing on key words
SPEAKING	Parts 3 and 4: decision-making

Reading and Use of English

Clothing and shopping vocabulary

1 Give the class a couple of minutes to find the pairs of adjectives, then elicit the answers plus their meanings. Students may need to use their dictionaries for *clashing*, *matching* and *patterned*. Suggest that they note down the pairs of opposites in their vocabulary notebooks.

> **Answers**
>
> casual – formal, clashing – matching, cool – unfashionable, loose – tight, patterned – plain, simple – sophisticated, smart – untidy

2 Elicit the adjectives from the class, checking the spelling of those that change or drop letters in the adverb form (*untidily*, *unfashionably*). Point out that we often say *fashionably dressed*, but *tidily dressed* is less common.

> **Answers**
>
> brightly, casually, formally, plainly, simply, unfashionably, untidily (*and possibly* coolly)

3 Students can do this activity in pairs or small groups. Allow them a few minutes to describe the people and clothes in the photos, answering any questions students may have about the names of garments or accessories.

4 Suggest that students look up any of the (mostly B2-level) italicised expressions that are new to them, then let them talk together for a few minutes.

5 Where possible, students use the contexts as clues to the meanings of these mainly B2-level expressions, but they can if necessary check with their dictionaries. Go through the answers, pointing out that students will see some of the expressions again in the Reading text.

> **Answers**
>
> 1 *out of stock* – not available in a shop; *in stock* – available in a shop
> 2 *a bargain* – on sale for less than its real value; *poor value for money* – costs more than it is worth
> 3 *exchange* – take it back to the shop where you bought it and change it for something else; *a refund* – money given back to you because you are not happy with something you have bought
> 4 *launched* – made available to customers for the first time; *sold out* – no more left to buy
> 5 *imports* – buys products from other countries; *exports* – sends goods to other countries for sale
> 6 *false* – not real; *genuine* – real
> 7 *budget* – very cheap; *uncompetitive* – worse than other prices, services or salaries
> 8 *consumers* – people who buy goods or services for their own use; *dealers* – people who trade in something
> 9 *shopkeepers* – people who own or manage a small shop; *suppliers* – companies that sell something
> 10 *purchases* – things people buy; *sales* – number of items sold

6 If you think the class would like to discuss these questions in some detail, let them work in pairs. Otherwise elicit the answers and discuss briefly. If nobody suggests *buyer for shops*, mention it to the class as this is the topic of the Reading text.

> **Suggested answers**
>
> designers, models, stylists, hairdressers, make-up artists, buyers

Part 6

7 Refer the class to the first point in Quick steps and explain that understanding text development, a useful reading sub-skill in itself, can often help locate the most likely parts of the text for the missing answers. Encourage students to do this as part of their gist-reading in future. If you feel that going through the answers now would make the exam task too easy, leave it until after they have finished the exam task.

> **Answers**
>
> 1 f 2 e 3 a 4 c 5 d 6 b

8 Tell students to do this quickly, as they will not have much time in the exam. Get them to note down the linking words if you don't want them to write in the book. You may prefer to leave checking their answers until after they have finished the exam task.

> **Suggested answers**
>
> B like that C This D This means E That (+ it, it's)
> F in that way G Consequently, like those

9 Allow 20 minutes for the class to do the exam task, working in exam conditions.

10 Give the class an extra minute or two for this, but remind them that in the exam they will need to do it very quickly. Then go through the answers. You may also want to focus on a range of linking expressions, e.g. *on the other hand*, *consequently*, as well as those they highlighted in Exercise 8.

Position of adverbs of manner and opinion

11 Remind the class that they studied the position of time adverbials in Unit 1 and adverbs of degree in Unit 3. Give students, working in pairs, a few minutes to find the adverbs in the text. Elicit that adverbs can be positioned either at the beginning, middle or end of a clause and that commas are used with adverbs of opinion (*unfortunately*, *Obviously*, *sadly*) to show that they apply to the whole clause or sentence.

Answers

it <u>quickly</u> takes off and sells really <u>well</u>
they won't let us stock them, <u>unfortunately</u>
<u>Obviously</u>, you need to be really enthusiastic.
think <u>carefully</u> about the target customer
Most of them, <u>sadly</u>, fail in their first year.

12 Some of the mistakes are quite basic, but are still quite common. Allow a few minutes for students to correct the mistakes, or elicit the answers directly from the class, making sure that they give all the variations.

Answers

1 do not speak English well
2 I very much like doing sports *or* I like doing sports very much
3 I had carefully read the store's catalogue. *or* I had read the store's catalogue carefully.
4 thankfully they believed me *or*, thankfully, they believed me *or* they believed me, thankfully
5 get to know the city better
6 send an email very quickly to the seller *or* send an email to the seller very quickly *or* very quickly send an email to the seller
7 naturally I have *or* , naturally, I have *or* I have a bicycle, naturally
8 I learned that I hadn't passed the examination, unfortunately *or* I learned that unfortunately I hadn't passed the examination *or* I learned, unfortunately, that I hadn't passed the examination

Listening

Part 3

1 🔘 **2.14** Begin by eliciting the pronunciation of some of the words, especially *catalogue*, *debt* and *guarantee*, which all have silent letters, and word stress, e.g. <u>check</u>out, <u>cata</u>logue. Then get students to work together in pairs to complete the text, using their dictionaries if necessary, though the contextual clues should help with these mainly B2-level expressions. Then play the recording once or twice, again highlighting the pronunciation of the words mentioned above.

Recording script

I always try to get everything I need for the week down at the shops and supermarket at the big shopping mall on the outskirts of town. At the supermarket, I fill up my trolley with my favourite items of food, sometimes choosing a different brand from the one I usually buy if it happens to be on offer, for instance 'Buy 2 and get 1 free', or '20% off'. At the checkout I normally pay cash or by debit card rather than by credit card, as I don't want to get into debt by spending more than I can afford. Sometimes I call in at one of the other shops to buy something for the house, though for a big item I usually look it up in the catalogue first. I always check it has a good guarantee in case anything goes wrong after I've bought it.

Answers

1 mall   2 trolley   3 brand   4 on offer   5 off   6 checkout
7 debit   8 debt   9 catalogue   10 guarantee

2 Give students a few minutes to discuss the picture in pairs, monitoring to check their usage and pronunciation, and giving feedback before they go on to the exam task.

3 Allow less than a minute to answer the question, then check the answer.

Suggested answer

their experiences when shopping

4 🔘 **2.15** Give students a couple of minutes to underline the key words, then elicit some answers. Play the recording without pausing, in exam conditions.

Note: the speakers use *wish* and causative forms which will be used as examples in Grammar which follows.

Suggested answers

A more, than, intended   B good value   C someone else, angry
D make, for me   E Internet, first time   F tried, money back
G advertisement, not, truthful   H glad, alternative, paying

Recording script

You will hear five different people talking about shopping experiences. For questions 1–5, choose from the list (A–H) what each speaker says. Use the letters only once. There are three extra letters which you do not need to use.

Speaker 1

I was in the computer shop looking for a new printer when a fantastic-looking laptop caught my eye. It was a completely new model, and although it was no bargain I bought it there and then instead of the printer, paying by cheque. The day after, though, I saw exactly the same model on sale in the supermarket, but for 150 euros less! I'd hardly used mine, so I took it back to the shop and asked for a refund, but the staff said they couldn't do that. I thought of stopping the cheque but that would've made them angry, and in the end I decided to keep the laptop. It runs well and I wouldn't be without it now, though I wish I still had those 150 euros, too.

Speaker 2

I always pick up a few things at the weekly street market, and last Wednesday I saw some interesting-looking items on a stall there and asked the seller how much they were. One in particular, a beautiful patterned vase, seemed very expensive and I didn't have enough cash on me, but the friend I was with lent me some, saying I could pay her back later. Delighted with my purchase, though worried in case I'd paid too much, I took it home and looked carefully at it. To my surprise there was a signature on the base, and when I looked it up I realised I had a genuine antique, worth far more than the man had charged me. I bet he'd be quite upset if he knew.

Speaker 3

I'd been looking for a cabinet that would fit the shape of the bathroom wall, so when I saw one advertised at the furniture store I raced round and paid cash for it. But I wish I'd been more careful measuring the wall because when I got home I found the cabinet was actually half a centimetre too wide. Furious with myself, I went back to the store and asked the salesman whether they had a slightly smaller one in stock, but they didn't. I could've got my money back but I knew that it was just the kind of cabinet I needed, so when he suggested having one made to fit exactly I agreed straightaway, though it meant handing over more money.

Speaker 4

I'd bought loads of stuff online before without any problems, so I wasn't pleased when I received an email saying that I still owed a seller for three blouses. She was quite reasonable about it, but I knew I'd only ordered one and it hadn't arrived yet anyway. I was just about to send her an angry reply saying she could keep the blouse and I'd keep my money, when there was a knock at the door. The postman handed me a large package, and inside were the three most gorgeous blouses I'd ever seen. I tried one on, and it fitted me as if I'd had it made to measure. I knew instantly that I wouldn't be sending any of them back, and later I sent the seller a payment for all three.

Speaker 5

By the time I reached the checkout queue I'd spent over an hour shopping and my trolley was full of the usual stuff. For once I hadn't seen any special offers but everything I'd picked up was essential, though I should've realised the total bill would be a bit higher this time. Because when at last I'd got to the counter and all my fish and fruit and veg and everything had gone through, my debit card was declined. It was just as well I had cash on me or else I would've held up all the other customers waiting behind me, and I know how annoying that can be. Just the other day I was saying how I wish people would check they have enough money before they go shopping.

Exam task answers

1 F   2 B   3 D   4 A   5 H

5 When the class have made sure that they have answered all the questions, elicit the answers.

Grammar

Review of *wish* and *if only*

1 Focus attention on the extracts from the recording in Listening. Elicit the verb form that follows *wish* in each case. Point out that *if only* is slightly more emphatic than *wish*, and less common – although it could have been used in the three extracts. The class should be familiar with these forms, but you may want to ask some concept questions to check, e.g. first extract: *Did the speaker have 150 euros? Does he have 150 euros now? Is he happy about the present situation?* Divide the class into pairs. Give students a couple of minutes to answer the questions (you may want to make sure that they realise that *I'd* in the second extract is *I had*), then go through the answers, eliciting more examples of each of the three types. Explain that we don't use *would* (third extract) in the first person, though we can use *could*, e.g. *I wish I could fly*.

Answers

1 b (past perfect simple)   2 c (*would*)   3 a (present simple)
4 all of them

2 Explain that the corrections all involve making changes to the verbs that follow *wish* or *if only*, and give students a couple of minutes to correct the mistakes. Go through the answers, explaining where necessary why the original forms were wrong. Point out that in sentence 2 *could* indicates that they can't do it, whereas *would* implies that they won't.

Answers

1 wish you'd / you had been   2 could find *or* would find
3 wish I'd / I had bought   4 wished I hadn't answered
5 If only I had known   6 you would come   7 wish I could spend
8 wish I hadn't decided to wear

3 Give students time to think about what they would say and to write their answers, encouraging the use of *wish* more than *if only*. Point out that in some cases there are several possible answers, but two will do. Go through the answers, checking particularly for accuracy in the use of verb forms after *wish* and *if only*.

Suggested answers

2 I wish I'd bought the shirt on Friday. If only I hadn't waited until Monday.
3 I wish I hadn't come here on a Saturday. I wish people would stop pushing.
4 If only I didn't have to go to work tomorrow. I wish I could go to the sales.
5 I wish she wouldn't keep borrowing my things. I wish she would ask me before borrowing my things.

Review of causative *have* and *get*

4 If the class seem unsure of the causative form, give more examples such as *I'm going to have my hair done, we're getting the house painted*. Point out that it may be possible to add an agent, e.g. *by a professional*, but usually it is unnecessary. Also explain that we normally use *have*, not *get*, when something unpleasant happens to us. Give students a few minutes to complete the rules, then check the answers. Elicit more examples, reminding students that *get* is more informal than *have*.

Answers

1 no   2 *have*   3 past participle

5 Give pairs or students working on their own a few minutes to complete the sentences, then check the answers.

> **Answers**
>
> 1 have ... repaired *or* get ... repaired   2 having ... wasted
> 3 'll/will have ... cut *or* 'll/will get ... cut   4 have ... cleaned *or*
> get ... cleaned   5 have ... tested *or* get ... tested
> 6 have ... delivered *or* get ... delivered

Optional activity

As a quick drill, get the class to answer the following questions using *have* or *get* plus the correct form of the verbs in brackets.

Why do people:

1 employ a gardener? (cut)

2 go to a dry cleaner's? (clean)

3 pay a photographer? (take)

4 take their car to a garage? (service)

5 send their children to school? (educate)

6 go to the dentist? (fill)

> **Suggested answers**
>
> (*get* also possible)
> 1 to have (*or* get) the grass cut   2 to have their suit cleaned
> 3 to have their picture taken   4 to have it serviced
> 5 to have them educated   6 to have a tooth filled

6 This activity could be done in pairs. Students discuss the questions using *have* or *get*. You may want to give some prompts, e.g. *I'd like to have my hair done every day*, *my clothes washed*, *my meals made*, *my appointments made*, etc. Monitor pairs for accuracy, then elicit some examples from the class.

> **Suggested answers**
>
> have my hair styled differently every week, have an expensive suit made, have my room tidied, have some exotic dishes cooked, have my appointments booked

Speaking

Parts 3 and 4

1 🔘 *2.16* This activity could be done in pairs. Give students a couple of minutes to complete the summary or note down the list of expressions, then play the recording once for students to check their answers. Then go through the answers with the class. If you want to choral drill the intonation, play and pause the recording at suitable points.

> **Recording script**
>
> To bring the conversation towards a conclusion, you can say *Which do you think would be best?* or *So which shall we choose?*, and to try to reach a decision you can use expressions such as *Well, are we both in favour of this one?* or *Shall we go for those two, then?* If you both decide on the same one or ones, say something like *Right, we're agreed* or *OK, those are the ones we'll go for*, but if you can't reach a decision, just say to your partner *Let's just agree to disagree* or *Let's leave it at that*.

2 Give the class a few seconds to read the exam task instructions, then elicit the answers.

> **Answers**
>
> six things
> 1 talk together about what might be good or bad about buying things in each of these shops
> 2 decide which two are the best to go shopping in

3 Put the class into groups so that students are not with their usual partners. Make sure that everyone knows what they have to do, then give them four minutes to do the exam task. Then, staying in the same groups, they go straight on to Exercise 4 where they will do Speaking Part 4.

4 Make sure that the 'examiners' and 'candidates' keep the same roles for Part 4. Tell the examiners to ask follow-up *Why?* questions where necessary. Time the groups so that they speak for no more than four minutes.

5 Students stay in their groups. Remind them of the importance of being polite and constructive in any criticism, and giving equal measures of praise to both candidates. Encourage them to comment particularly favourably on the use of expressions from Exercise 1.

6 Students repeat Parts 3 and 4, and again give feedback at the end. You may want to have a class round-up at the end to discuss any difficulties that may have come up.

Reading and Use of English

Phrasal verbs with *out*

1 Point out that this is also good practice for understanding phrasal verbs in longer texts, e.g. Reading and Use of English Part 1. Students then do the exercise in pairs. You may want to elicit one or more sentences with each verb as you go through the answers, making sure everyone understands the exact meaning.

> **Answers**
>
> 1 finished the supply of, none left   2 get rid of   3 have none left
> 4 see what it's like   5 get   6 doesn't come into the house
> 7 are found   8 be unavailable, no more to buy

2 Students complete the sentences. Check their answers, then elicit at least one more example with each phrasal verb.

> **Answers**
>
> 1 breathe out   2 rushed out   3 cross (it) out   4 back out
> 5 shut out   6 worn out

Part 4

3 Give the class a minute or two to study both sentences, then elicit the answers.

> **Answers**
>
> *I should've* (*gone*) → *wish I'd* (wish + past perfect), *gone for a ride on it* → *tried out* (phrasal verb with *out*): *I'd / I had | tried out*

4 Give students, working on their own, a minute or two to note down the focus of each sentence quickly. You may prefer to leave going through the answers until they have completed the exam task. The class do the exam task individually, writing just the missing words, not the whole sentence. Allow about 10 minutes, as in the exam.

> **Answers**
>
> 1 *wish*   2 causative *have*   3 *wish* + phrasal verb
> 4 *if only* + phrasal verb   5 causative *get*
> 6 *wish* + causative *have*

> **Exam task answers**
>
> 1 wishes she hadn't / had not | spent   2 may have your luggage | searched   3 I hadn't / had not | stayed out   4 hadn't / had not | (been) sold out *or* run out   5 I'll get it | sent   6 'd had / had had his tyres | checked

5 Give the class a minute to check for content and language accuracy, then elicit the answers. Ask students which words in each answer they think score a mark.

Writing

Extreme adjectives

1 This activity could be done in pairs. The extreme adjectives presented in this exercise are all B2 level, but you may want to begin by giving or eliciting further, low-level examples, e.g. *big – huge*, *unhappy – miserable*. Students do the matching, using their dictionaries if necessary. Check the answers. Explain that some of these adjectives are used in particular ways, as they will see in the next exercise.

> **Answers**
>
> angry – furious, big – massive, bright – vivid, pleasant – delightful, silly – absurd, strange – bizarre, suitable – ideal, surprising – breathtaking

2 Get students to work out the meaning of the adjectives, then check the answers.

> **Answers**
>
> all 'very good' except *disgraceful*, *dreadful*, *severe*

3 Point out that answers meaning 'good', e.g. 5 and 8, will have more possible answers than most of the others. Give the class two or three minutes to answer these, then check.

> **Answers**
>
> 1 furious   2 vivid   3 absurd, bizarre   4 ideal   5 breathtaking, stunning, superb   6 dreadful   7 severe   8 stunning, fine

Part 1 essay

4 Begin by referring the class back to the Writing Part 1 advice in Units 3 and 6, also the Quick steps in Unit 1 *Writing Part 2 informal letter* and the Writing guide on page 88. Then allow a minute for them to study the instructions, before going through the answers.

> **Answers**
>
> 1 You have been talking in your English class about the advantages and disadvantages of buying things on the Internet rather than getting them in the shops.
> 2 write an essay for your English teacher
> 3 which is cheaper, and easier

5 Give students plenty of time to find the things, then check the answers.

> **Answers**
>
> 1 disagrees, 5th paragraph
> 2 Note 1: 3rd paragraph – young people may not have debit or credit cards, card details can be stolen
>   Note 2: 2nd paragraph – goods may be late or not arrive, buyer has to post faulty or unsuitable items back
>   Note 3: 4th paragraph – going to the shops can be fun, you can try clothes on
> 3 a also, In conclusion
>   b however, On the other hand, though, in contrast
>   c Increasingly, Certainly, Worse still
>   d massive, enormous, tremendous
>   e having your purchases delivered, having your card details stolen

6 Encourage students to use extreme adjectives and opinion or degree adverbs where possible, and also *wish* for the last point. Allow 30 minutes for the actual writing, in exam conditions. Remind students to leave time for checking at the end.

> **Model answer**
>
> I don't agree that shopping online is better than going to the shops. It is certainly not easier for anyone without a computer or for those with limited computer skills. However, I do feel that sometimes shopping online is the only real option.
>
> When choosing clothes and books, I don't always know exactly what I want to buy beforehand. I like to browse before making my choice. In clothes shops, you can try things on. And in bookshops, you can browse the shelves and displays, and choose something that appeals to you. I accept that shopping online is generally cheaper, but in my view the extra expense I may incur is worthwhile.
>
> So when is online shopping the only option? Here's an example. My father loves opera. However, the major music store in my city has recently closed down and the others only have a small selection of opera CDs. My father has had no choice but to buy his CDs online.
>
> In conclusion, I would always choose to go shopping if this option is available to me.

Revision

1 | **Answers**

1 'd bought   2 were   3 'd waited   4 didn't   5 lived
6 hadn't   7 would   8 wouldn't

2 | **Answers**

1 I hadn't / had not | thrown out *or* thrown away   2 wish they
wouldn't | try   3 have this skirt | completely altered *or* altered
completely   4 hadn't / had not | run out of   5 could have my
clothes | ironed   6 only we'd / we had | been able

3 | **Answers**

Get is also possible in all these answers.
2 You should have it mended. *or* Why don't you have it
mended? *or* How about having it mended?
3 You should have it filled. *or* Why don't you have it filled? *or*
How about having it filled?
4 You should have it (dry) cleaned. *or* Why don't you have it
(dry) cleaned? *or* How about having it (dry) cleaned?
5 You should have it cut. *or* Why don't you have it cut? *or*
How about having it cut?
6 You should have them taken. *or* Why don't you have them
taken? *or* How about having them taken?

4 | **Answers**

Across
1 item   4 off   8 dealer   9 loose   10 label   13 stock
16 casual   17 match   15 debit
Down
2 mall   3 bargain   5 false   6 cool   7 trolley   8 debt
11 bright   12 launch   13 sales   14 brand   15 plain

Remind students that there is more practice on the CD-ROM.
Also encourage them to do Practice test 2 on the website.

Writing guide answer key

Part 1

Essay

1 1 your English class has been discussing studying and jobs

   2 whether it is better to go into higher education rather than get a job straight from school

   3 your teacher

   5 which has immediate advantages, which is better for your career, your own idea

2 1 fairly formal – no contracted forms, formal linking expressions, impersonal tone (until the conclusion)

   2 short introduction, arguments 'for' getting a job straight from school in one main paragraph, arguments 'for' going into higher education in another, concluding paragraph

3 1 second paragraph

   2 first part of third paragraph

   3 second part of third paragraph

4 in favour of going into higher education

Part 2

Letter

Exam task A

1 1 an email from your penfriend; informal

   2 an email in reply; your favourite kind of food, where you would like to eat, where you would like to go afterwards

   3 your penfriend Lena

2 1 yes – informal: *Hi*, expressions such as *Many thanks*, conversational *Yes*, exclamation marks, contracted forms, informal ending, etc.

   2 yes

   3 accepts invitation: first paragraph; says what her favourite kinds of food are: second paragraph; says which kind of restaurant: third paragraph; suggests somewhere to go afterwards: fourth paragraph

Exam task B

1 1 a job advertisement; (fairly) formal

   2 a job application; whether you: are interested in clothes and fashion, have a good level of English, have experience of selling in shops

   3 Mr James O'Neill, the manager

2 1 yes – formal: *Dear Mr*, no contracted verb forms, complete and complex sentences, *Yours sincerely*, etc.

   2 yes

   3 says she is interested in clothes and fashion: second paragraph; says she has a good level of English: fourth paragraph; says she has experience of selling in a shop: third paragraph

Article

1 1 an interesting place / a place worth visiting

   2 travel magazine, readers of that magazine

   3 describe the place, say what you most remember about your visit there

2 1 neutral – use of contracted forms but also complex complete sentences

   2 the first two paragraphs describe the place, the last two deal with the writer's visit

   3 the location, appearance and dimensions of the rock; how long people have lived near it; legends surrounding it; the route to the top of it; the variations in temperature, flora and fauna; the views from the top

   4 He appears to find it very interesting, though at the end he wonders if the legend had a basis in fact.

Report

1 1 a public park near your home

   2 your teacher

   3 give a brief description of the park, say what people can do there, recommend some improvements

2 1 formal – no contracted verb forms, passive verb forms, complex sentences

   2 Main features – brief description of the park, Leisure facilities – what people can do there, Conclusion – recommend some improvements

   3 the park should be looked after a little better, more sporting activities should be made available

Review

1 1 a swimming pool in your area

   2 an English-language website, visitors to your country

   3 describe the pool, say what you think of it, say whether you would recommend it to other people

2 1 b   2 a   3 d   4 c

Workbook answer key

READING AND USE OF ENGLISH

Part 7

1 people talking about their friends

2 four

3 which person says, thinks or does each of the things

4 ten

Exam task

1 B   2 D   3 C   4 C   5 A   6 A   7 D   8 D   9 A   10 B

Grammar

1 1 I belong   2 when you arrive   3 *correct*   4 we spend
   5 When you receive   6 needs   7 it is becoming
   8 *correct*   9 I'm / I am applying   10 who drive

2 1 'm/am taking   2 's/is getting   3 ends   4 own
   5 'm/am seeing   6 'm/am trying   7 rises
   8 hear

LISTENING

Part 1

question 1: 1 one, **2** female, **3** she is talking about her new bedroom, **4** what she likes / her opinion

question 2: 1 two, **2** one male, the other probably female (normally, if there are two speakers they are different genders), **3** on a bus, **4** a place

question 3: 1 one, **2** male, **3** one half of a phone conversation, **4** reason/function

question 4: 1 two, **2** one female, the other probably male, **3** an interview, **4** job / line of business

Exam task

1 A   2 B   3 A   4 C

Recording script Track 2

You will hear people talking in four different situations (in the exam you will hear eight). For questions 1–4, choose the best answer (A, B or C).

1 You hear a teenager talking about her new bedroom.

It might not be the perfect room, for instance it's a bit too narrow for a really large bed, but I'd rather have this one than either of the other two in the house. <u>The wallpaper and paint are really bright and they make it feel bigger than it really is, which is just as well</u> because it has these rather old-fashioned wardrobes and cupboards that take up a lot of space. They certainly wouldn't be my choice if I were buying bedroom furniture, but I suppose I'll get used to them eventually.

2 You overhear a conversation on a bus.

Woman: Aren't you getting off at the next stop?

Man: You're right, that's where I usually get off for the office, but it's early so I thought I'd stay on as far as the High Street and do a couple of things there.

Woman: Some shopping?

Man: Yes, <u>after I've taken this back. I've just finished the last chapter and it's a few days late so I'll have to pay a fine</u>, but it was worth it.

Woman: Hmm, I must <u>take that out</u> myself sometime. Which shop are you going to?

Man: To the bookshop, as it happens. To pick up a copy of that new Steve Jones novel.

3 You hear a man talking on the phone.

When I got home this evening there was a note waiting for me saying that your company had called round with the new washing machine I'd ordered, but there was nobody in. To be honest I hadn't expected you to be so efficient, so when the salesman asked me when it could be delivered I just said 'anytime'. <u>I realise I should've made it clear I'd be out in the afternoon, and I hope that didn't cause too much inconvenience.</u> I'll be at home all day on Friday if you can bring it round then.

4 You hear part of an interview with a businesswoman.

Man: So tell me, have you always been in the hiring business?

Woman: Yes, originally it was motor vehicles such as cars and vans, but it was getting more and more difficult to compete with the big international car-hire firms so <u>two years ago I switched to two wheels</u>.

Man: And has that gone well?

Woman: Yes, there seems to be plenty of demand for bikes round here, and particularly in the current economic situation a lot of people are looking for <u>something that uses less fuel</u>, and of course is much easier to park.

READING AND USE OF ENGLISH

Part 3

1 1 worried   2 stressed   3 attractive   4 terrified
   5 unacceptable   6 surprising   7 crowded   8 enjoyable
   9 disorganised   10 impressive

2 1 adjective   2 what causes a feeling   3 -ing

Exam task

1 tiring   2 sociable   3 increasingly   4 worrying
5 enthusiastically   6 anxious   7 impractical *or* impracticable
8 cautious

WRITING

Part 2 informal letter

1 1 Sam, an English-speaking friend

   2 a relative of yours who you see a lot, why you enjoy being with him or her

3 Though, sister's, quite a bit, we're, !, So tell me, a lot, –, Hope to hear from you soon.

2 1 yes, in the second paragraph

  2 after *in the holidays* and before *We've got* so each paragraph answers one of the questions

  3 yes: begins *Hi* + first name, informal words (e.g. *Thanks, nice, great, get on, kids, love, fantastic*), contracted forms (e.g. *It's, sister's*), punctuation (!, –), no personal pronoun (*Hope*), short sentences, friendly tone, simple linking words (*and, but, though, because*), ends *Bye for now*, then first name only

  4 a older that/than, **b** we're seeing / we see, **c** mountain biking without *the*, **d** ~~excited~~ exciting, ~~competitious~~ competitive, ~~sympatic~~ sympathetic

  5 Suggested answers: close friendship, get on really well, We've been friends since we were, things in common, something I really like about, whenever, In short

2 Eating and meeting

LISTENING

Part 2

1 artist Leonie Meyer, making new friends online

2 1 adverb *or* adverbial phrase **2** number *or* distance
  3 noun **4** noun *or* adjective **5** noun *or* verb
  6 adjective **7** month *or* adjective **8** noun *or* noun phrase
  9 noun *or* noun phrase **10** noun *or* job

Exam task

1 alone *or* on her own *or* by herself **2** 60/sixty kilometres/km
3 Internet (connection) **4** friendship **5** walking **6** friendly
7 May **8** sense of humour **9** hills **10** farmer

Recording script Track 3

You will hear artist Leonie Meyer talking about making new friends online. For questions 1–10, complete the sentences.

A question I'm sometimes asked is why I chose the Internet as a way of making new friends. Well, most people are surrounded by colleagues or fellow students or whoever, and they naturally tend to form friendships within that group, but for (1) someone like me whose job means I'm alone most of the time that obviously doesn't happen. And that's particularly the case now I'm living in a cottage in a remote part of the countryside.

I remember thinking when I first saw the place that there couldn't be a town within 50 kilometres. Actually (2) it must be over 60, because it's 30 kilometres to the river, and that's not even halfway. It takes ages to get there. But it's got all the features of a modern house, and it was like that when I moved in. It had all the basics like water and electricity, and there was already a surprisingly good mobile phone signal, but (3) I did have to have an Internet connection installed. That works well, it's very fast and reliable, and I soon decided to use it to find a new friend.

I wasn't interested in dating, and I'd thought of putting my details on a social networking site like Facebook, but in the end (4) I went for a friendship one because I was only really looking for one or two friends. When I registered I had to say what kind of person I was looking for, in terms of their interests, so I mentioned my work, but it was never really my aim to meet another painter because that might restrict the conversation to art, which I didn't want. Instead (5) I gave walking as my favourite hobby, and said I hoped it would be a shared interest.

I also listed the types of music I like, where I like travelling and so on, and also gave a brief description of my personality. I wasn't sure what to say about myself but in the end (6) I put 'friendly', though my brother said anyone who chooses to live that far from civilisation should be considered 'highly unsociable'! He was joking, though, and I was quite looking forward to people getting in touch via the site once I'd I signed up in March last year. Then in April there were a couple of messages from people who turned out to be wasting my time, so (7) it was May before I heard from anyone I felt I wanted to correspond with. That was Hannah, who's now become one of my best friends.

Sometimes you feel immediately that you have things in common with someone you meet, but actually the first things I noticed with her were the ways we differ, such as our ages – she's quite a bit older than me – and also the fact that she's from a much wealthier background. But gradually (8) I realised her sense of humour was just like mine, and we began to chat online with each other more and more often, until eventually we agreed to go for a walk together.

She lives about ten miles away and has her favourite walk there, by the lake, whereas I like to go up and down the river valley near here. So we agreed to compromise and (9) nowadays we walk in some hills that lie about halfway between the two, several times a week. We get on really well, and have some great chats, and laughs.

I've made other friends online, too. For instance there's Nina, who I met for the first time just the other day. It turns out she lives quite near here, which was a nice surprise. (10) She's actually a farmer these days, after some years working as a company lawyer in the city. She much prefers the country life, and I must say so do I.

Grammar

1 1 noticed **2** was snowing **3** kept **4** had already gone
  5 had fallen **6** wasn't going **7** used to be
  8 seemed **9** 'd been **10** was pedalling **11** 'd been riding
  12 crashed **13** realised **14** 'd cut **15** walked **16** could
  17 led **18** watched **19** did **20** decided

2 1 I had lost **2** asked **3** wrote *or* used to write *or* would write **4** had started **5** didn't use to eat **6** was climbing **7** had decided **8** included **9** had lived *or* had been living **10** had disappeared

READING AND USE OF ENGLISH

Part 2

1 factual and historical

2 Chinese, Egyptian, Indian, Greek

3 1 preposition **2** preposition **3** auxiliary verb
  4 relative pronoun **5** adverb **6** preposition
  7 auxiliary verb **8** verb

Exam task

1 to **2** from **3** had **4** which **5** why **6** for **7** would
8 took

Vocabulary

1 shape **2** heart **3** fed **4** alone **5** proposed
6 attracted **7** ease **8** nerves **9** side **10** touch
11 company **12** sight

WRITING

Part 2 article

1 **1** to take part in a competition in an international magazine,
with the aim of having your article chosen as one of three
for publication

2 the food, the occasion

3 neutral, neither too formal nor too informal

2 **a** paragraph 3

b paragraph 4

c paragraph 1, paragraph 2

3 **1** The moment **2** Once **3** before long
4 in the meantime **5** simultaneously

You would be right to say, you may not be surprised to hear

3 Getting away from it all

LISTENING

Part 3

1 five people talking about a journey they have recently made

2 **A** arrived late **B** friend, drove **C** glad, expensive ticket
D didn't feel safe **E** enjoyed, conversation, passenger
F marvellous view **G** ate well, during
H should, different, transport

Exam task

1 F **2** H **3** G **4** A **5** D

Recording script Track 4

*You will hear five different people talking about a journey they
have recently made. For questions 1–5, choose from the list
(A–H) what each speaker says about the journey. Use the letters
only once. There are three extra letters which you do not need
to use.*

Speaker 1

There was a strong wind when we took off so the plane was
shaking a bit and some passengers were obviously getting
scared, but I'd flown in much worse conditions and I wasn't
bothered. For much of the flight (F) <u>I spent my time admiring
the mountain scenery</u> from 10,000 metres, or whatever height
we were above those peaks. We were served a tasteless
sandwich, which compared unfavourably with the delicious-
looking hot meal being served to the lucky few in first class. I
know flying is bad for the environment, but when you live on an
island there really is no alternative unless you fancy spending
hours on a ferry. And in a storm like that that really can be
scary.

Speaker 2

It was midwinter and it'd seemed a good idea at the time to
take the train rather than go by car. As I bought the tickets
online at home I thought about relaxing while I ate a tasty meal,
admiring the beautiful countryside from the window, and maybe
even having a good chat with an interesting stranger sitting
next to me. But in the event the window was too dirty to see
through, the food tasted like cardboard and the man in the next
seat spent the entire journey snoring loudly. The train got in on
time, but long before then (H) <u>I was wishing I'd driven instead</u>,
whatever the risk of hold-ups and accidents that might have
involved.

Speaker 3

It'd been a pretty good crossing for the first couple of hours,
but then the waves got much bigger and the ship started rolling
around. It wasn't that I was worried it would sink or anything
like that, but I did regret (G) <u>having that excellent meal when
I first came on board</u> as I began to feel quite seasick. That
uncomfortable feeling in my stomach lasted the whole voyage,
and I was relieved to see the harbour eventually appear in
front of us, even though it was in a rather unattractive port city.
Fortunately we got in well ahead of schedule, no doubt assisted
by the very strong wind blowing in the same direction as us.

Speaker 4

I was meeting my parents at the airport and as it would've
taken nearly three hours by train I took a cab instead. It was a
long way on boring motorways through dull countryside and
I thought I might regret going by road, but I had such a good
chat with the driver that the time just flew past. Which was
just as well because we were held up for ages in a really bad
jam, and despite all the driver's best efforts – without taking
any risks, I should add – (A) <u>we were never going to make it on
time</u>. To make matters worse my parents' flight arrived early,
but at least they were able to have a good meal at the airport
while they waited for me.

Speaker 5

As a student I'd done that overnight bus journey before and I
knew how boring it was. Outside there was wonderful tropical
scenery but it was dark all the way, and of course you don't
get a meal on a coach. It was just as well I'd had that fantastic
curry before setting off. At least, though, I thought to myself,
it was safer than going in a friend's car. Until, that was, a huge
lorry suddenly cut in front of us and (D) <u>for a moment I wished
I'd put my safety belt on</u>. I mentioned this to the guy next to
me but he just nodded. He wasn't very friendly, and I was glad
when we finally pulled in at the bus station right on time.

Grammar

1 **1** may, might **2** don't have to, needn't **3** could, might
4 can, could **5** can't, mustn't **6** should, ought to
7 didn't have to stay, didn't need to stay **8** can't, couldn't

2 **1** b **2** c **3** b **4** a **5** c **6** a **7** b **8** a

Vocabulary

1 **1** in response to **2** in need of **3** obsessed with
4 fed up with **5** had nothing to do with **6** conscious of
7 capable of **8** supposed to be **9** With regard to
10 familiar with

2 Across

3 client **9** shrink **11** scheme **12** process **16** major
18 founder **19** actively

Down

1 resource **2** factor **4** feature **5** seek **6** assess
7 waste **8** distant **10** impact **13** concern **14** standard
15 promote **17** host

READING AND USE OF ENGLISH

Part 1

1 b

2 **1** adverbs **2** nouns **3** prepositions **4** prepositions
5 nouns **6** adjectives **7** adverbial phrases
8 prepositional phrases

Exam task

1 D **2** B **3** A **4** C **5** D **6** C **7** D **8** A

WRITING

Part 1 essay

1 **1** You have had a discussion in your English class; you
have been talking about the advantages and disadvantages
of having a tourist industry that involves building in
beautiful parts of the country.

2 your teacher

2 **1** *which is better for the country's economy*: third paragraph
which is better for local people: second paragraph
your own idea: fourth paragraph

2 firstly, then, in addition, last but not least

3 They've – They have, if you ask me – I believe/think
or In my opinion, messed up – destroyed/ruined, 100s
– hundreds, e.g. – for instance / for example / such
as, Loads – Much/Most, etc. – and so on / and similar
vehicles, should've – should have

4 the three points that are given in the notes, with reasons

4 Taking time out

READING AND USE OF ENGLISH

Part 6

1 storytelling is becoming more popular again, especially
among young people

2 Suggested answers
B the (musician), he **C** The (group), the next decade
D this **E** Unlike all those kinds **F** Since then, it
G back then, them, he

Exam task

1 F **2** C **3** D **4** A **5** G **6** B

Grammar

1 I have already booked **2** dislikes living **3** enough time to go
4 I have just bought **5** finish working *or* work

6 I haven't yet seen *or* I still haven't seen
7 too far for us to walk **8** regretted sending
9 miss watching **10** for some years

READING AND USE OF ENGLISH

Part 4

was becomes negative, *too* changes to *enough*, *late* changes to
early, *too* goes before *late* but *enough* follows *early*

Exam task

1 went on | to do (*once* + past perfect)

2 never forget | visiting Hollywood (*always remember*, noun)

3 refused to | let photographers take (*said … couldn't take*)

4 have been waiting here | for (past simple, *ago*)

5 not cheap enough | for students (*so … that*)

6 hasn't / has not managed to | become (*succeeded in* + *-ing*)

LISTENING

Part 4

1 **1** a radio interview **2** Lily Alonso **3** a singer

2 **B** See recording script below.

3 Suggested answers
1 relax **2** What, practise **3** Why, look, stage
4 Which, herself **5** difficult, decide **6** wears, lucky
7 best, drink

Exam task

1 A **2** C **3** B **4** B **5** A **6** A **7** B

Recording script Tracks 5 and 6

*You will hear a radio interview with singer Lily Alonso. For
questions 1–7, choose the best answer (A, B or C).*

Interviewer: I'm very pleased to have with me this afternoon
Lily Alonso, and I'll be asking her about how
she prepares for a concert. The first and most
obvious question, Lily, is whether you get a bit
tense before you perform?

Lily: It depends when and where, really. If you're
talking about several hours ahead of a show then
yes, I often am. Though once or twice I've felt
quite confident at that point because it's a place
I'd played before and the show had gone well.
But (example) if you mean when I'm just about to
go on stage, then I'm probably a bit fed up with
hanging around, and I just want to get on with it
and see how it goes.

Interviewer: Do you have any particular way of making
yourself feel more relaxed?

Lily: In my early days I was in a band and we were
always telling each other jokes and having a good
laugh, and that certainly helped. But now I'm solo
(1) I spend a few minutes taking some calm, slow
breaths, not too deep. I've heard yoga helps, too,
though I've never actually tried it.

Interviewer: And on the day of the show, do you practise
everything on the stage first?

Lily: (2) <u>I always go there but just to get the feel of moving around it, making a mental note of how many steps I can take in any direction</u>. I want songs to sound fresh when I do them, which they don't if you've been singing them all day. And I find the quickest way to forget the words is to keep trying to remember them.

Interviewer: What do you do after that?

Lily: I often go and take a seat in one of the front rows, where the audience will be watching me in the evening.

Interviewer: Why do you do that?

Lily: I try to imagine myself up there later on, giving a really great performance, fans clapping and cheering, things like that. Whether or not that actually happens (3) <u>it certainly makes me feel I can do it, and that's the important thing</u>. Then I go back to my dressing room, which is usually nice and quiet, and get ready.

Interviewer: Do you have people to help you with that?

Lily: Well, I normally have my make-up done for me, and – if they need doing – my nails, too. Someone always used to do my hair for me, too, but I was never entirely happy with the way it looked so (4) <u>nowadays I tell them I'd rather they left it to me</u>.

Interviewer: And how do you decide what to wear?

Lily: Some things are easier to choose than others. Shoes, for instance. I have my favourite pair and that's that. For trousers, too, I know pretty well in advance which I'm going to wear on any given night. But (5) <u>I've got so many T-shirts that there are times I can't make my mind up and I get one of the assistants to pick one</u>.

Interviewer: Do you ever wear anything that brings you luck? I ask because quite a few performers I've spoken to seem to do that.

Lily: Yes, I know what you mean. One of the girls I used to sing with simply wouldn't go on stage without her lucky earring. Just one – she'd lost the other, unfortunately. (6) <u>In my case it's a bracelet</u>, though for years I always wore a special necklace that I was convinced brought me good luck during live performances.

Interviewer: And one final question, what do you drink before you perform?

Lily: Well, sometimes when you're tired in the middle of a tour you're tempted to have a nice cup of coffee, but that's not good for your voice because it dries out your mouth and throat. Tea and cola are also best avoided for the same reason, whereas milk leaves a thin layer of fat there which doesn't help either, though (7) <u>that can be cleared by having a glass of freshly-squeezed lemon or orange. So that's what I'd recommend</u>. Or, if it's not available, just a simple glass of water.

Interviewer: Thank you, Lily. And good luck with your next tour.

Lily: Thanks.

Vocabulary

Across

2 step   3 count   5 based   8 play   9 kept   11 rely

Down

1 focus   2 sat   4 jump   6 depend   7 carry   10 turn   12 log

WRITING

Part 2 review

1   **1** a cinema which you have visited recently

  2 on a website that compares entertainment facilities

  3 describe the cinema, say what you think of the cinema, recommend or not recommend it to others

2   **1** a second,   **b** fourth,   **c** first,   **d** third

  2 fairly formal / neutral

  3 watch films at the Odeon, but only during the week; take your own refreshments, rather than buy them there

3   a fine *or* superb building, a fine *or* superb sound system, a breathtaking experience, customer service there is poor, the queues to get in are dreadful, which is absurd nowadays

5 Learning and earning

READING AND USE OF ENGLISH

Part 7

1   **1** a magazine article

  2 four university students describing how they became interested in particular subjects when they were at school

  3 what these students did, felt and thought

2   Suggested answers

  2 surprised, quickly, time   **3** mysterious event

  4 enjoyed, few people   **5** later, specialise, subject

  6 lesson, interesting   **7** difficulty, decision   **8** book useful

  9/10 background research

Exam task

1 D   **2** B   **3** A   **4** B   **5** A   **6** C   **7** C   **8** C   **9/10** A/D

Grammar

1 homework   **2** help   **3** *correct*   **4** knowledge   **5** *correct*
6 advice   **7** rubbish   **8** leisure   **9** earnings   **10** *correct*

READING AND USE OF ENGLISH

Part 3

1 a student thinking about possible future jobs

2   **1** uncountable   **2** singular (there is no plural form)
  3 the suffix -*ation*

Exam task

1 advice   **2** historians   **3** employers   **4** possibility
5 researcher   **6** fascinating   **7** librarian   **8** trainee

LISTENING

Part 2

1 fashion photographer Aldo Lombardi, Aldo's work

2 **1** noun **2** place **3** time **4** noun **5** (uncountable) noun
6 (uncountable) noun **7** place *or* city **8** noun
9 noun **10** number

Exam task

1 wedding **2** home **3** nearly a year *or* almost a year
4 (fashion) magazine **5** variety **6** communication
7 New York **8** websites **9** contacts **10** 20/twenty

Recording script Track 7

You will hear fashion photographer Aldo Lombardi talking about his work. For questions 1–10, complete the sentences.

Even as a kid I was always the one with the camera, whether I was out with the family at the seaside or on a school trip. But (1) it wasn't until I took some wedding pictures that I realised that was what I wanted to do for a living. It was the feeling of capturing the emotion of the occasion that did it for me.

I suppose I would like to have gone to a photography school, but my family couldn't afford it so (2) I did a 12-month online course instead, learning technical skills in my own home. That was good in some ways, though I missed out on things I would've learnt if I'd been at college. Or at university doing a photography degree, which would be a possibility these days.

I'd also rather optimistically assumed I'd just walk into a job within a few days of completing the course, but six months went by and I was still applying for work and being rejected, and (3) after nearly a year of that I was on the point of giving up when a firm at last agreed to take me on. I must say that was quite a relief.

I'd sent most of my applications to national agencies providing photographers for social occasions and schools, but (4) the one that turned out to be successful was to a fashion magazine. I had to be trained on the job, of course, though that would also have been the case if I'd been taken on by a newspaper, say, or a marketing organisation. And I really enjoyed the work, right from the start.

Sometimes I'm asked what my favourite aspect of it is, and certainly the money's pretty good, but (5) it's the fact that there's so much variety that really makes it worthwhile. In a typical day, for instance, I might spend time on the phone talking to clients to get an idea of their needs, find a suitable location for the photo session, rent any equipment we need, then set up lighting and backgrounds. And that's before I've actually taken any photos.

Of course, doing that well is the main skill you need in this job. But you also have to give the people you're photographing clear instructions and advice if you are to get the shot just right, so (6) there always has to be effective communication between you and them. If you're self-employed you also need good business skills, but of course that's not my case. Not yet, anyway.

One day, though, I'd like to work for myself, so that I could choose which city to work in rather than have that decided by the magazine. Obviously Milan or Paris would be great places to be, but (7) it's always been my dream to be based in the English-speaking world. It'd be a difficult decision but if I had to choose I think my preference would be for New York rather than London. Sydney comes a close third, by the way. I really like Australia.

And photography is definitely a profession with a future. Employment of photographers in the USA, for instance, grows about ten per cent every year, and although the decline in newspaper sales may lead to fewer jobs in the press, (8) this will be more than made up for by websites.

My advice to a young person thinking of becoming a photographer would be to consider going to a photography school, or doing a degree in photography – even though I didn't do either. Times were different then. And although I got lucky in the end, I did spend a long time looking for my first job. At a school you'd be meeting lots of people in the industry, (9) building up useful contacts for the future. And of course you'd also be learning from experts, experimenting with the latest equipment and so on.

Finally, if you're someone who's actually looking for a job as a photographer, remember that the most important thing is to show potential employers what you can actually do. So when you're applying you should send perhaps fifteen but (10) certainly no more than twenty examples of your work. Sending in thirty or forty photos, for instance, risks giving the impression you don't know how to edit your own work, which doesn't look good from the employer's point of view. Oh, and make sure they really are your best ones. Not just your favourite holiday pics.

WRITING

Part 2 formal letter of application

1 **1** helping children enjoy themselves on a summer adventure camp

  2 whether you want to spend a month doing this, whether you like camping and outdoor activities, whether you have a good level of English

  3 say why you would be suitable for the work

  4 Mr O'Leary, formal

2 **1** yes **2** yes **3** a–e yes to all **4** yes **5** no **6** no – too informal

3 Suggested replacements:

Dear Mr O'Leary,

I have just seen your **advertisement** in the **newspaper** and **I am** writing to apply for a job on the summer camp.

I am aged 18 and **I will** be leaving school this summer. As **I have** studied English for several years my level is **quite good**, and I hope to pass Cambridge First when I take it later this year.

I have a lot of experience of looking after **children, especially** the age group mentioned, because for the last two years **I have** been helping to organise trips to the countryside for inner-city children. As well as that, I have three brothers and sisters **who are all considerably** younger than me.

I also **very much** like going camping and taking part in a wide range of sports and activities, **such as** walking, rock-climbing and canoeing, and **I am** a qualified swimming instructor.

Please find enclosed my CV / curriculum vitae. I am available for interview **at any time**, and **I look forward to hearing from you.**

Yours sincerely,

Alexia Kallis

---

6 Getting better

LISTENING

Part 1

question 1: **1** one, **2** female, **3** talking about a recent holiday, **4** reason

question 2: **1** two, **2** male and female, **3** conversation, **4** agreement

question 3: **1** one, **2** male, **3** talking about a journey, **4** place

question 4: **1** two, **2** one male and the other probably female (normally, if there are two speakers they are different genders), **3** conversation with a doctor's receptionist, **4** purpose/function

Exam task

1 B   **2** A   **3** B   **4** C

> **Recording script Track 8**
>
> *You will hear people talking in four different situations (in the exam you will hear eight). For questions 1–4, choose the best answer (A, B or C).*
>
> *1 You hear a woman talking about a recent holiday.*
>
> Things started going wrong from the start, when the cab turned up late at our house. We nearly missed the plane because of that, and I'm going to complain to the taxi firm. The flight was delayed, too, and when we landed one of our cases was missing. Also, <u>the accommodation at the resort was completely inadequate for two people, with no view at all from the window. The brochure was full of lies and I'm determined to get our money back</u>. Oh, and as soon as we got to the beach it started to pour with rain, which made us even angrier. Though I've got over that now because I suppose it could happen anywhere.
>
> *2 You hear a teenage boy and his mother talking.*
>
> Boy: I can't go to school today, Mum. I've got flu.
>
> Woman: You certainly don't look very well, but I'm not sure it's flu. <u>It's probably a cold</u>, though I know that can be nasty, too. You most likely caught it watching football the other day, surrounded by all those people coughing and sneezing.
>
> Boy: I definitely caught it at school, Mum. And anyway I'm going to see another match on Saturday. I'll be better by then.
>
> Woman: Oh, we'll have to see about that. If you're not well enough to go to school, then I'm not having you sitting around in that freezing stadium. That'd just make it worse, whatever it is you've got.
>
> Boy: <u>I think it *is* just a cold, Mum, actually.</u>
>
> *3 You overhear a man talking about a journey.*
>
> I do this route quite often and normally it leaves on time, more or less. Though I suppose in the middle of winter you have to expect the occasional delay here, in the same way that the trains get held up by ice on the lines or the planes by fog on the runway. Actually, it's probably fog that's holding things up for us right now. I heard on the radio before I came out that there are some massive <u>jams</u> this morning, so even when we do eventually get moving we'll probably find that it's <u>slow going</u>, especially as the <u>rush hour</u>'s now about to start.

> *4 You hear a man talking to a doctor's receptionist.*
>
> Man: Yes, I was here last week. The doctor gave me a prescription and advised me to take things easy. But now I feel even worse, so <u>I wonder if there's any chance I could have a word with her later this morning?</u>
>
> Woman: I'm afraid not. <u>She's fully booked</u> until this afternoon.
>
> Man: Not even five minutes? I'm incredibly busy at the moment and I really can't come all the way back here after lunch.
>
> Woman: Maybe if the doctor told you to take it easy you shouldn't be working quite so hard. That might be part of the problem.
>
> Man: Yes, I know it's probably my fault, but this couldn't have come at a worse time for me at the office.

Grammar

1 **1** *correct*   **2** who *or* that   **3** which   **4** tennis,   **5** *correct*   **6** whose   **7** On the 20th of July, when you return, we   **8** *correct*   **9** mother, who lived miles away, nobody   **10** where

2 **1** where   **2** , who is a nurse,   **3** which *or* that   **4** when I was in Tarifa   **5** who *or* that   **6** when   **7** , which is now empty,   **8** whose   **9** , where it is always cold,   **10** , whose brother also plays in the team,

Could be left out: 3, 6

Vocabulary

1 **1** rang up   **2** speak up   **3** healed up   **4** ran up   **5** tidy up   **6** speed up   **7** stayed up   **8** eat up   **9** used up   **10** dress up

2 **1** athlete   **2** cyclist   **3** diver   **4** footballer   **5** golfer   **6** gymnast   **7** rider   **8** sailor   **9** skier   **10** surfer

READING AND USE OF ENGLISH

Part 2

Exam task

1 when   **2** whose   **3** up   **4** who   **5** as   **6** on   **7** where *or* when   **8** doing

WRITING

Part 2 letter

1 **1** a part of a letter from Ethan, an English-speaking friend

2 reply to Ethan's letter in 140–190 words in an appropriate style; write about either playing or watching the sport you most enjoy

3 informal

2 **1** five   **2** playing it   **3** **a** fourth, **b** second, **c** third

3 **1** **a** It was great to hear from you.

b I'm very well too, thanks

c Looking forward to hearing from you again.

2 pass – give the ball to someone else, bounce – make a ball move up after hitting the ground, shoot – try to score a goal, kit – clothes and equipment, rule – what you must or mustn't do in a game

3 to prepare, to answer, to keep fit, so that everyone gets involved

4 which, who, which,

5 *yes:* Hi, great, thanks, right now, Anyway, get stronger, lots of, Do try, love it, Looking forward, All the best; *contracted forms* (I'm, It's, don't, there's, you'll); *punctuation (dash, exclamation mark)*

7 Green issues

READING AND USE OF ENGLISH

Part 6

1 **1** no   **2** yes

2 **2** It seems to be taking place   **3** It has existed
   4 In fact   **5** –   **6** Now
   B Because, this   **C** But, these   **D** It   **E** it, that   **F** these
   G This, it

Exam task

1 D   **2** B   **3** G   **4** E   **5** A   **6** C

Vocabulary

1 acid rain   **2** animal conservation   **3** carbon emissions
4 climate change   **5** global warming   **6** industrial waste
7 melting icecaps   **8** oil spills   **9** renewable resources
10 solar power   **11** tropical storm   **12** greenhouse gas

LISTENING

Part 3

1 jobs in nature conservation

2 **A** unpaid overtime   **B** chose, so, friend   **C** began, university
   D upsetting   **E** leave, become, police   **F** sad, trees, dies soon
   G wanted, since, young   **H** volunteer before

Exam task

1 D   **2** G   **3** H   **4** A   **5** C

Recording script Track 9

You will hear five different people talking about their jobs in nature conservation. For questions 1–5, choose from the list (A–H) what each speaker says. Use the letters only once. There are three extra letters which you do not need to use.

Speaker 1

After completing my degree I went into teaching for a while, and I'm now a nature reserve manager – which isn't a position I ever imagined myself having when I was a kid. The hours can be long, but I do get a bonus for working evenings. One of my responsibilities is to watch out for people damaging the reserve in any way. That can range from picking wild flowers and letting dogs run free, to illegal hunting and deliberate starting of fires.

(D) That happened last year and the effect on local wildlife was something I hope I'll never have to see again. Actually, the police are now training us in information-gathering and observation techniques, and even showing us how to set up our very own crime scene investigations, so we're doing what we can.

Speaker 2

(G) I suppose I've never really considered any other career. The idea of it was a childhood dream and that's never changed, so I'm really lucky to be doing this, especially as I'm not a graduate. I was actually going to do a degree in biology, like my best friend Marcos, but I didn't want to have to take out a loan to pay for my studies. Of course the job has its disadvantages, such as being outdoors in the middle of winter or working on Saturdays for very little extra pay, but it's rewarding in other ways. This week, for instance, I'm taking care of some old trees in the park. These are really old: they've been around for several hundred years and will last a lot longer if we look after them properly.

Speaker 3

Since the Wildlife Association took me on, I've been involved in a project to convert an area of farming land into a nature reserve. I know one or two farmers weren't happy about losing part of their land, but most local people are in favour of the changes we're making, which include planting bushes and wild flowers, forming lakes with islands, and generally creating a place for birds, animals, fish, insects and other creatures to live. It's a great job to have, not just because you're doing something worthwhile, but because you often make friends with your colleagues. (H) It's best to have experience before you apply, which is why I first did unpaid work for a year, helping to clean up beaches near my home town.

Speaker 4

Nowadays the majority of people working in nature conservation have diplomas or degrees, but I was the exception, going straight into full-time employment from school. I remember as a kid my schoolfriend Eva Martin used to talk about working with nature, and later on she did actually look at the possibility of working in conservation. But although she decided in the end it wasn't for her, she suggested I might be suited to it. And I'm so glad she did, because although (A) the salary's quite low and stays the same no matter how many extra hours you put in, I've thoroughly enjoyed every minute of it, even when I've found myself working well into the evening.

Speaker 5

For the last six months I've been carrying out a wildlife survey, observing how some creatures have increased in number while others have declined. For instance, there are fewer deer round here than there used to be, and although some people are rather upset about that, the fact is that those which remain are much healthier. (C) I actually graduated in environmental conservation just last year and was taken on here straightaway, which was ideal because I love spending my time outdoors. It's a wonderful job, so good that I would probably still do it even if they didn't pay me. But please don't tell my employers that!

Grammar

1 if I had more time   **2** *correct*   **3** If you hadn't helped
4 we would never have got   **5** *correct*   **6** *correct*
7 I wouldn't be in hospital now   **8** *correct*   **9** if I hadn't made
10 *correct*

READING AND USE OF ENGLISH

Part 4

1 second conditional   **2** comparative   **3** mixed conditional
4 comparative   **5** phrase with 'in', -*ing* form of verb after
preposition   **6** third conditional

Exam task

1 less meat | if I were   **2** aren't / are not as | good as *or* not
so | good as   **3** if | they hadn't / had not taken   **4** much more
pleasant | than   **5** a/its part in | reducing   **6** if they hadn't /
had not | assisted

WRITING

Part 1 essay

1 **1** you have had a class discussion on the harm cars do to the
environment

   2 your teacher

   4 convenience for travellers, reducing the use of fuel, your
   own idea

2 **1** quite formal, yes

   2 for: second paragraph; against: third paragraph

   3 note 1: third paragraph; note 2: second paragraph; safety
   and security

   4 own opinion: fourth paragraph

3 **1** Nevertheless   **2** Whereas *or* While   **3** whereas *or* while
   4 On the other hand   **5** Despite

8 Sci & tech

READING AND USE OF ENGLISH

Part 5

1 addiction to using electronic devices, its consequences, and
current research into it

2 no

Exam task

1 C   **2** D   **3** A   **4** B   **5** C   **6** A

Grammar

1 **1** the United States   **2** for a swim   **3** *correct*
   4 a very nice person   **5** waste energy   **6** *correct*
   7 the environment   **8** I am a student   **9** the civilisation
   10 all inventions

2 **1** The prize was given to a girl from my school.

   2 The public must be told about the danger.

   3 Has your computer been repaired yet?

   4 Business messages used to be sent by fax.

   5 It is thought that sales are still increasing.

   6 The story has been denied by the government.

   7 The Atacama Desert is believed to be the driest in the
   world.

8 A new study will be carried out by a team of scientists.

9 It is reported that millions of computers were affected.

10 Scientists are believed to have discovered a new type of
plant.

READING AND USE OF ENGLISH

Part 1

1 b

2 **1** computer   **2** word processing, music player
   3 the Internet   **4** web page   **5** computer   **6** drive
   7 line   **8** the Internet

Exam task

1 D   **2** B   **3** B   **4** C   **5** A   **6** C   **7** A   **8** B

LISTENING

Part 2

1 **1** a scientist, Alistair McGregor

   2 a Dark Sky Park in Scotland where people go to look at
   the night sky

2 **1** –   **2** –   **3** a year   **4** an area   **5** a (large) number
   6 –   **7** a fraction or percentage   **8** –   **9** –
   10 a period of time

Exam task

1 light pollution   **2** birds   **3** 2009 / two thousand (and)
nine   **4** 750 / seven-fifty / seven hundred (and) fifty
5 7,000 / seven thousand   **6** satellites   **7** $^3/_4$ / three-quarters
8 (popular) (scientific) magazines   **9** a (small) torch
10 15/fifteen minutes

Recording script Track 10

*You will hear scientist Alistair McGregor talking about a Dark
Sky Park in Scotland where people can look at the night sky.
For questions 1–10, complete the sentences.*

One aim of Dark Sky Parks is to create the ideal environment
for people to study the night sky, with or without telescopes,
and to bring that about (1) we need to keep light pollution to
an absolute minimum. That's why they tend to be well away
from cities and lit-up roads, for instance. Other key objectives
include energy saving, and protecting wildlife from the effects
of night skies that are too bright.

And that can affect many creatures' habits. You only have to
think of how lights in your home can attract unwanted insects.
More seriously, (2) a bright sky can lead to birds singing all
night, instead of waking up at dawn and starting to sing then.
That can make them too tired to feed normally the next day.

Now the park I'd particularly like to talk about is the Galloway
Dark Sky Park in Scotland. It was actually the first to be
(3) set up in Europe, back in 2009, although the world's very
first Dark Sky Park opened in 2006 in the state of Utah, USA.
There was also another set up in Pennsylvania in 2008, and a
couple of years later Europe's second park opened, in Hungary,
though it's not as extensive as the Galloway one. Whereas the
Hungarian dark sky park is just over 100 square kilometres,
(4) the Scottish one covers around 750. Having said that, the
Hungarians are now planning to open a second one that's 820
square kilometres, and some of the new ones in Canada are
very big, too.

The wonderful thing about all these parks is that you can see things that just can't be seen elsewhere. To start with, a massive number of stars. On TV the other evening they were talking about being able to see over 10,000 there, and although I don't think you'd actually ever see that many, (5) there certainly may be up to 7,000 visible on a very clear night. You'd also see several planets, plus the moons and rings of the biggest ones.

Of course, you'd need a good telescope to spot things like those, though even with the naked eye there's a lot to see. The planet Venus, for instance, is very bright, and you may be able to spot satellites, too. Some of them are as bright as anything in the sky, but unlike stars or planets, for instance, (6) they may cross the part of the sky visible to you in a matter of minutes. Sometimes the light from them seems to flash, which also makes them different from other objects in space.

I'm often asked when's the best time to see the night sky in a park such as Galloway Forest, and the answer is: in winter. That far north, of course, it only gets dark for a few hours in mid-summer. You also have to remember you won't see much (7) when there are clouds in the sky, which weather statistics show is the situation there just under three-quarters of the time, day and night. And on around a quarter of the clear nights there's a bright moon that can make viewing difficult, so you have to plan your visits carefully. It's important, too, to take a good chart showing the positions of the stars in the night sky. Textbooks have them, of course, but they tend to be rather small and difficult to read when you're on a dark hillside. The same applies to those in newspapers, published at the beginning of each month, so (8) one of the popular scientific magazines is probably the best place to get a decent-sized one.

Even so, something like that may still be quite hard to follow at night, especially as you're probably avoiding nights with moonlight, and starlight is very weak. So (9) it's best to take a small torch with you. That's certainly better than using the interior light in a car or, worse still, turning on the headlights, as I've seen some people do. It must be really annoying for others there. And not only that, (10) it also spoils your night vision for around 15 minutes, as your eyes have to get used to the dark all over again. Which is quite a long time if, as often happens, there's a partially cloudy sky and you only get half an hour or so total viewing time in the whole night.

WRITING

Part 2 article

1 **1** an English-language magazine called *Home Life*

 2 it will be published next month

 3 how people's homes will be different in the future, and how they might remain the same

2 **1** yes – it is the correct length; the content is relevant to the topic: the two main paragraphs describe the possible differences, then say what will remain the same

 2 yes – the beginning asks the reader a question, then answers it in the main paragraphs; the ending makes the reader think back to the main content

 3 overall, yes – it is neutral in style, using complete sentences, passive forms and formal linking expressions, but also several informal linkers and a personal feeling (*I wish I could*) at the end

---

3 articles: a/one hundred years, to school, on a computer *or* on the computer, kind of online education

 spelling: temperature, climate, programme (program), automatically, possible

 the expression *Well, I suppose that …* – the sentence could begin *Almost everything …*

9 Fame and the media

LISTENING

Part 4

1 singer Alisha Ryan, talking about fame

2 **1** realised, wanted, famous, when **2** How, feel, result
 3 What, newspapers say **4** What, regret **5** most, money
 6 What, enjoy **7** What advice, friends

Exam task

1 C 2 A 3 B 4 B 5 A 6 B 7 A

Recording script Track 11

You will hear an interview with singer Alisha Ryan, in which she talks about fame. For questions 1–7, choose the best answer (A, B or C).

Interviewer: Today's guest is singer Alisha Ryan, who I'm sure you will remember was the winner of a well-known TV talent show a few years ago, and she'll be talking to me about fame. Tell me, Alisha, was becoming a famous singer something you'd always wanted to do?

Alisha: Not really, no. As a child I dreamt of becoming a model, though I grew out of that in my teens. I'd always enjoyed singing, of course, but (1) the idea of becoming a star never occurred to me until I saw Katie Wyatt, who'd been in my class back in my school days, in a talent show. To be honest, she wasn't much good, and my brother said, 'You've got a better voice than her,' and I suddenly knew it was something I at least had to try to do. The boy I was going out with at the time wasn't exactly keen on the idea, but my mind was made up. And he soon became an ex anyway.

Interviewer: And how did you feel when you first went on live TV, and you had that victory?

Alisha: Well, I didn't actually sing that well. I was annoyed with myself and I think my family and friends were a bit disappointed with my performance, too. (2) At one point I was convinced I'd lost, so afterwards I was just glad when the scores were announced and it became clear I hadn't. I didn't even feel like celebrating much.

Interviewer: Though you did in fact become a celebrity overnight.

Alisha: Yes, I realised that the next morning, when the national press had all this stuff about me.

Interviewer: I imagine they said a lot of nice things.

Alisha: Yes, though (3) <u>it was mostly about how I had the right look, how stylish my clothes were and that sort of thing</u>, rather than how I'd actually performed or what they thought of my singing voice. But at least there was none of the criticism they directed at the others, especially one guy who said something very rude to the judges.

Interviewer: I think in general the media treated you quite well, didn't they?

Alisha: More or less, yes. Though that only lasted a year or so.

Interviewer: What went wrong?

Alisha: Well, that boyfriend I mentioned said some stupid things about me cheating on him to a tabloid – I don't know how much they paid him – and (4) <u>I just said 'no comment', because none of it was true. Which was a mistake,</u> because the next thing I knew they'd put that stuff onto their front page, followed by 'And Alisha doesn't deny it!' Worse still, they kept calling round at my parents' house asking for their reaction, which my mum and dad found really upsetting.

Interviewer: And what happened after that? Did you continue to be successful?

Alisha: Oh yes, for quite a while. They say there's no such thing as bad publicity and my songs, both on CD and as downloads, started selling better than ever. Though you only make any real money out of those if you write them yourself, which I don't. I also had plenty of work touring round the country and abroad, but (5) <u>it was the income from sponsors, particularly clothing and make-up manufacturers, that I was mainly relying on.</u> And when that started to decline quite sharply the following year I realised it'd soon be over for me, at least as an A-list star.

Interviewer: And you didn't mind that?

Alisha: Yes and no, really. On the one hand (6) <u>it was good having plenty of money and a personal assistant to look after day-to-day matters for me,</u> and it might have been nice to have been on the cover of a fashion magazine – not that I was ever actually asked to – but I never had much interest in things like invitations to 'hard to get into' nightclubs. And I didn't really become close friends with anyone I met then.

Interviewer: How do you feel about friendships among celebrities? Is it always a bad idea?

Alisha: I wouldn't say that exactly. You're bound to meet some good people in that world, and if you do then it's fine to be friends. But not just as a way of giving your career a boost. And remember (7) <u>it's probably going to end sometime, and when it does you'll want to go back to those you were close to before you were famous, so don't lose touch with them.</u> It's amazing how many people never think about that.

Interviewer: Thank you, Alisha.

Grammar

1 he would come
2 whether they had
3 insisted on getting
4 Laura had done it
5 we would go, the night before
6 threatened to kill
7 what had happened … had taken
8 invited me to have
9 said that I had helped him
10 reminded him not to take off his jacket

Exam task

1 Chloe whether she | could sit
2 where we would stay | that
3 told Helen | not to look
4 threatened to shoot | them both
5 offered to fix | my TV *or* our TV
6 whether/if she would | lend him *or* to | lend him

1 **Across**
  1 ability   5 reduction   7 death   8 proof   10 viewer
  11 admiration

  Down
  1 amusement   2 intention   3 assistance   4 length
  6 depth   9 heat

2 1 arrangements   2 least   3 preference   4 disappearance
  5 contribution   6 frozen   7 coincidence   8 introduction
  9 variety   10 identification

READING AND USE OF ENGLISH

Part 3

serious papers and tabloids

Exam task

1 choice   2 decision   3 variation(s)   4 agreement
5 distinction   6 preference   7 attention   8 height

WRITING

Part 2 report

1 1 you have had a class discussion about the possibility of setting up a new college magazine
  2 your teacher
  3 say whether the magazine should be published on paper or online; what sections it should contain; and how often it should be published
  4 neutral or fairly formal

2 1 aim   2 majority   3 carried   4 challenge   5 step
  6 sum   7 recommendation   8 recommend

3 1 Introduction, Form, Contents, Frequency, Conclusion
  2 yes

3 online, with a hard-copy edition for those without computers; college news, photos of recent events, calendar of upcoming events, editorial column plus letters to the editor, puzzles and quizzes; preferably weekly

10 Clothing and shopping

LISTENING

Part 3

1 people talking about their jobs in shops, supermarkets or department stores

2 **A** pay, good salary, work   **B** buy things, cheaply
C customers, children   **D** times, don't have much to do
E better job, soon   **F** good communication
G customers, annoy   **H** like, hours vary

Exam task

1 D   **2** B   **3** H   **4** F   **5** G

Recording script Track 12

You will hear five different people talking about their jobs in shops, supermarkets or department stores. For questions 1–5, choose from the list (A–H) what each speaker says about their work. Use the letters only once. There are three extra letters which you do not need to use.

Speaker 1

I work in a small shop at the station, between platforms three and four. We sell the kind of things that passengers need: newspapers and magazines, snacks, drinks, and so on. It gets busy, of course, during rush hours; (D) far less so mid-morning and mid-afternoon, and I often end up reading one of the magazines to pass the time. I'd actually like to work more flexible hours and I'm hoping to talk to my boss about that, but otherwise it's not such a bad job to have. For instance, I can travel free on local trains early morning and late evening. And most customers are quite friendly, though as they're usually hurrying to catch a train there isn't much time to chat with them.

Speaker 2

I've always loved books so for me a bookshop is the ideal place to work, really. Not that I have time during the day to read them, but I do get a chance to see all the latest titles as stock comes in, and (B) there's quite a generous discount for employees. The hours suit me too, as I have to be home at the same time each day for the kids when they get back from school. I suppose the only thing I miss about my old job – I was a representative – was persuading people to buy things and achieving sales targets, which I really enjoyed. Though of course some customers could be rather rude and annoying, something that never happens where I work now.

Speaker 3

The supermarket where I work is open 24/7, so (H) the shifts change quite often. Some of the staff can't stand that, but the lack of routine actually suits me. It's quieter there at night, of course, although that doesn't mean I'm any less busy because at those times there are fewer checkouts open. One or two of the customers can get a bit impatient if there's a long queue, but I don't let that bother me and I just ignore them. I'm not paid enough to get upset about things like that, and I don't

even get anything off when I buy my own food there. If I could find a better job I'd probably take it, but there's no chance of that at present.

Speaker 4

I work six days a week, nine to five, and I wish I didn't have to. Just the occasional early finish would be nice. Apart from that, though, it's a nice job to have if you're interested in clothes, as I am. It's only a small shop in a very big mall, but there's a steady stream of customers and (F) I always seem to get on well with them. Which is essential in this kind of work, because very often they don't know exactly what they want, or else the things they're trying on make them look ridiculous, and you have to advise them, gently, without hurting their feelings. I buy most of my own clothes there, too, even though the firm no longer gives staff any price reductions.

Speaker 5

Working in a department store has its good points and its not-so-good ones. There's no overtime, for instance, and there's never any time to get bored because there are always tasks like setting up displays if there aren't any customers around. Sometimes I actually prefer that, such as (G) when I'm not in the mood to hear complaints about the quality of the goods they've bought, as if I were somehow to blame. That can be quite irritating, and at times I've wondered whether I should try to get promotion. There would be other advantages like the higher salary, the flexible working hours and the large discounts on everything in the store. But I don't fancy the added responsibilities and in the end I've always decided to carry on doing what I'm doing now.

Vocabulary

1 **1** thrown out   **2** run out   **3** turned out   **4** backed out
5 sold out   **6** spell out   **7** stay out   **8** worn out

2 **1** delightful   **2** massive   **3** ideal   **4** furious   **5** stunning
6 bizarre   **7** absurd   **8** vivid   **9** dreadful   **10** fine

Grammar

1 **1** wish I could spend   **2** wish I'd / I had had   **3** *correct*
4 wish you had been able to   **5** that had never happened
6 *correct*   **7** wish people would take   **8** could have stayed
9 wish people would dress   **10** wish I could earn

2 Suggested answers
1 could play   **2** 'd/would give   **3** had   **4** didn't live
5 wouldn't play   **6** 'd/had gone   **7** could've / could have come   **8** 'd/had done

3 **1** I had   **2** get my computer repaired   **3** *correct*
4 have their car serviced   **5** *correct*   **6** not to have
7 *correct*   **8** *correct*   **9** must have their passports checked
10 had our photos taken with her

4 Suggested and example answers
1 How often do you have your hair done?
I have my hair done once a month.

2 When do you have your temperature taken?
I have my temperature taken when I have flu.

3 Would you like to have your room redecorated?
Yes, I would very much like to have my room redecorated.

4 Have you ever had anything stolen?

Yes, I had my phone stolen last year.

5 When do you have to get your passport stamped?

I have to get my passport stamped when I travel to another continent.

6 Do you think you will ever need to have a tooth taken out?

I hope I'll never need to have a tooth taken out.

7 Would you like to have any of your clothes made to measure?

Yes, I would like to have my suits made to measure.

8 Have you ever had your toenails painted?

Yes, I once had them painted pink.

READING AND USE OF ENGLISH

Part 4

1 causative *get* **2** *wish* + phrasal verb **3** causative *have*
4 *if only* **5** causative *have* **6** *wish* + phrasal verb

Exam task

1 to get those shoes | repaired

2 we'd / we had | set out *or* started out

3 had my wallet | stolen

4 only | I'd / I had seen

5 's/has had his application | rejected

6 had | turned out

WRITING

Part 1 essay

1 1 in your English class, you have been talking about how much people enjoy shopping; write an essay for your teacher, using all the notes and giving reasons

2 how much people spend, what they like to buy, your own idea

2 1 note 1: third paragraph; note 2: second paragraph

2 the power of advertising in a consumer society, and its effect on people

3 yes – quite formal

4 severe, massive, dreadful, absurd

Progress test 1 Units 1–2

1 Match sentence halves a–f with 1–6.

1 Please go away and leave
2 That man's loud voice is getting
3 I'm living abroad and I've lost
4 Everyone's away, so please keep
5 I love Jo, so I'm going to propose
6 I get very upset if a friend takes

a touch with my friends.
b me company.
c me for granted.
d me alone.
e on my nerves.
f to her soon.

2 Complete the dialogue with the correct form of the verbs in brackets. Use the present simple or the present continuous.

Marcos: Hi Felipe. **(1)** .... (you / get) this bus every day?

Felipe: No, I **(2)** .... (usually / take) the 64 to work, but I **(3)** .... (not / go) to the office today.

Marcos: Oh, why not?

Felipe: Well, I **(4)** .... (get) a bit tired of that job, and I **(5)** .... (think) of leaving soon. In fact, I'll do that as soon as I **(6)** .... (find) something better.

Marcos: **(7)** .... (the boss / know) you **(8)** .... (take) the day off today?

Felipe: Not yet. I'll call him later when he **(9)** .... (arrive) at the office. I don't like him very much. He **(10)** .... (always / criticise) the staff, and most of us **(11)** .... (not / deserve) that.

Marcos: It **(12)** .... (not / surprise) me that you want to leave.

3 Use a form of the word in capitals to complete each sentence.

1 Simon is very .... He feels he always has to win.   COMPETE

2 It was .... of you to eat all that cake and leave none for me!   GREED

3 Antonio always tells the truth, but I'm afraid Louis is rather ....   HONEST

4 That dog becomes quite .... whenever you walk past the garden.   AGGRESSION

5 I felt so .... that I went for a ten-kilometre run in the countryside.   ENERGY

6 It's .... to lend a lot of money to someone who you don't know.   FOOL

7 Seeing my sister again after so many years apart was an .... experience.   EMOTION

8 Jeff's motorbike is really .... It breaks down almost every day.   RELY

9 I really wanted to go surfing, but Chloe was less .... than me.   ENTHUSIASM

10 The shop assistant was .... so I demanded to see the manager.   HELP

4 Choose the correct alternative.

When I **(1)** *was / had been* just 16, my parents **(2)** *were telling / told* me that I would have to go to a new school, as they **(3)** *decided / had decided* to move to another town. For me it was a big change in my life, as I **(4)** *used to grow / had grown* up in that area and all my friends **(5)** *were going / went* to the same school. We also **(6)** *were spending / used to spend* a lot of time together in the evening, and since the previous summer I **(7)** *'d gone / 'd been going* out with a boy in the same class as me.

It was very difficult for the first few weeks after we **(8)** *had moved / had been moving*. I really **(9)** *would miss / missed* my friends, and every day I **(10)** *would send / was sending* an email or text message to at least one of them. At the same time, though, I **(11)** *was getting / used to get* to know some of my new classmates quite well, and by the time I **(12)** *was / 'd been* there a few months I **(13)** *used to begin / 'd begun* to make some good friends. It was at that point that I **(14)** *was realising / realised* that I **(15)** *moved / 'd moved* on from my old life, although I'll never forget my friends back in my home town.

5 Choose the correct word (a, b or c) to complete each sentence.

1 Some people .... meals and just have a coffee instead, which is very unhealthy.
   a chop
   b skip
   c slice

2 Can you please stop making that silly noise. It's really .... !
   a irritating
   b challenging
   c fascinating

3 A .... company provided all the food for my sister's wedding reception.
   a consuming
   b cooking
   c catering

4 Karl always thinks the worst will happen, and his brother is very .... , too.
   a optimistic
   b pessimistic
   c sympathetic

5 I feel more .... to work when I know that other people will benefit from what I do.
   a distracted
   b motivated
   c refreshed

6 You should try to have a more .... diet consisting of different kinds of healthy food.
   a balanced
   b organised
   c serious

7 Jenny is extremely .... , so you must be careful not to say anything that might upset her.
   a sensible
   b thoughtful
   c sensitive

8 That steak was so .... that I couldn't cut it with my knife.
   a tough
   b hard
   c ripe

Progress test 2 Units 3–4

1 Complete each sentence with one of these words and the correct preposition.

> ashamed capable familiar informed
> obsessed popular prepared supposed

1 Karen is .... everyone and she gets invited to lots of parties.

2 Most people wouldn't be .... working as hard as you do every day.

3 The boys are .... what they did and they promise never to behave like that again.

4 People aren't .... use mobile phones in that restaurant, but some do.

5 I'm not .... this machine. I don't know how it works.

6 I'm simply not .... lend Jeff any more money. He never pays it back.

7 We were not .... the firm's decision until we received an email last night.

8 Josh loves rock music. He's .... one band, in particular.

2 Choose the correct alternative.

1 After travelling for two days and nights, we were *very / completely* exhausted.

2 It was *absolutely / extremely* cold once the sun went down.

3 I think you were *rather / quite* right to continue your journey on your own.

4 It's getting *rather / completely* late, so I think I'd better go home.

5 My parents were getting *totally / a bit* worried when they hadn't heard from me for a week.

6 It was *quite / completely* late by the time we reached the theatre.

7 When the storm had passed, we could see that our tent was *extremely / totally* useless.

8 My girlfriend was *a bit / absolutely* furious when I didn't turn up at the cinema.

9 I didn't think that show was *completely / very* enjoyable.

10 We were all *slightly / really* delighted when that young singer won the competition.

3 Complete the text with the *-ing* or the *to* + infinitive form of the verbs in brackets.

I usually enjoy (**1**) .... (walk), but my day out with Jack was not a success. He had suggested (**2**) .... (spend) the day in the countryside and I had agreed (**3**) .... (go) with him, but I soon realised I had made a big mistake. We had decided (**4**) .... (set off) early in the morning and he had promised (**5**) .... (be) ready by eight o'clock, but when I called round at his house he was still in bed and at first he refused (**6**) .... (get up). I then had to wait while he got ready, and by the time he had finished (**7**) .... (have) breakfast it was well after nine and we didn't actually manage (**8**) .... (get going) until nearly ten. After 30 minutes' walking he said he needed to stop (**9**) .... (have) a break, and for the rest of the morning he insisted on (**10**) .... (do) that every half hour. By lunchtime I was starting (**11**) .... (wish) I had gone on my own, and when Jack admitted he'd forgotten (**12**) .... (bring) any food with him I really began to regret (**13**) .... (agree) to spend the day with him. I said I didn't mind (**14**) .... (share) my sandwiches with him, but he said he wanted a proper meal so then we had to try (**15**) .... (find) a café in a small town nearby. Eventually we found somewhere and he walked in. I just said 'Bye, Jack' and kept on (**16**) .... (walk).

4 Rewrite the sentences using *too*. Then write them again with *enough*.

> **Example:** It's so cold you shouldn't go outside.
> *It's too cold (for you) to go outside.*
> *It isn't warm enough (for you) to go outside.*

1 Your brother is very young, so he shouldn't travel on his own.

....

....

2 That team is so weak they won't win a single match.

....

....

3 We couldn't see anything because it was so dark.

....

....

4 The hotel was so expensive that we couldn't stay another night.

....

....

5 One runner was so slow that he couldn't keep up with the others.

....

....

6 Marion didn't sing well, so she didn't win a prize.

....

....

5 Complete the sentences with these words.

> expedition   hiking   hitchhiking   means
> tour   travel   trip   voyage

1 The .... across the Atlantic Ocean on a luxury liner lasted four days.

2 We did a quick .... to the seaside, coming back home the same day.

3 When our car broke down we tried .... , but nobody stopped for us.

4 My new job involves a lot of international .... , which can be quite exciting.

5 The first .... across the ice to the South Pole took place over 100 years ago.

6 I really enjoy .... through the countryside, well away from the roads.

7 Several .... operators organise holidays on those remote islands.

8 By far the best .... of transport to cross the desert is the bus.

6 Complete the sentences using *must (have)*, *might (have)* or *can't (have)* and the verb in brackets.

1 The lights are out and there's nobody around, so the show .... (finish) some time ago.

2 I don't know why our plane was late taking off, but it .... (be) because it was a bit foggy.

3 Carlota .... (leave) the hospital yet because she still hasn't sent me a text message.

4 I can't get a ticket for the concert anywhere. They .... (sell out) already.

5 I'm not sure where Emma went, but she .... (go) shopping because the sales are on.

6 Jake went away on holiday last weekend. You .... (see) him downtown yesterday.

7 At last the ski slopes are all open. It .... (snow) a lot last night.

8 I don't actually remember which road we took, but it .... (be) the A14.

Progress test 3 Units 5–6

1 Use a noun formed from the word in capitals to complete each sentence.

1 The 20 .... managed to swim to an island, and waited there to be rescued.   SURVIVE

2 I've always wanted to become a .... because I love books.   LIBRARY

3 The TV cameras focused on the .... as the presenter asked him a question.   INTERVIEW

4 In those days, the rich paid no taxes and had .... to do everything for them.   SERVE

5 We're looking for new .... who will put money into our football club.   INVEST

6 We'd better call an .... if the lights go out again.   ELECTRICITY

7 Our .... has told us we must get a lot fitter if we want to win matches.   TRAIN

8 One day I want to be a .... , so I'm learning how mechanical things work.   PHYSICS

9 One of the flight .... asked me to put my seat belt on before we landed.   ATTEND

10 Sports equipment .... hope the Olympics will increase sales of their products.   MANUFACTURE

2 For each of 1–15, choose from the three alternatives. In some cases, no relative pronoun is necessary.

The first time

The first time I went mountain biking was two years ago, **(1)** *which | – | when* I was seventeen. I was with some friends **(2)** *who | which | –* already had lots of experience, **(3)** *– | that | which* made me feel a little nervous. I was using a fairly old bike **(4)** *who | – | whose* my elder brother had lent me, and wearing a helmet **(5)** *that | who | –* was a little too big for me, **(6)** *– | that | which* is not a very good idea.

At first all went well as we rode up to the top of the biggest hill, **(7)** *– | where | which* all the best tracks started. I said to Jessica, **(8)** *whose | – | who* was riding alongside me, that it was much easier than I'd expected, but she told me that would all change in a minute, **(9)** *– | that | when* we began to go downhill.

She was right. Within seconds we were racing down a track **(10)** *where | – | that* led towards the bottom of a valley **(11)** *which | – | where* seemed to be covered in huge rocks. I couldn't believe how quickly I was going, but the others, **(12)** *which | whose | –* bikes were better than mine, were going even faster. I tried to catch up with them, but as I came into a bend **(13)** *– | that | where* was much tighter than I'd expected, my back wheel lost grip on the dusty surface and I went sliding across the ground until I hit a large rock. My left leg, **(14)** *that | which | –* was badly cut, was very painful. But when I saw the damage to my helmet **(15)** *– | which | that* caused by hitting that rock, I realised just how lucky I'd been.

3 Replace the verbs in *italics* using phrasal verbs with *take*.

1   I *started playing* volleyball when I was at secondary school.

   ....

2   I found it hard to *understand completely* the fact that I'd won the gold medal.

   ....

3   I'll have to *obtain* a loan from a bank to pay for my studies.

   ....

4   A foreign billionaire has *got control of* our football club.

   ....

5   The arts festival has really *become a big success* since the media started covering it.

   ....

6   If you *accept* more responsibilities at work, you expect to be paid more.

   ....

7   At first I wasn't sure if I liked Laura, but now I've *started to like* her a lot.

   ....

8   The local restaurants always *employ* more staff in the summer months.

   ....

4 Complete the dialogues with phrasal verbs. Use the correct forms of these verbs plus *up*.

clear   heal   speak   speed   split   use

1   'That was a nasty cut on your knee. How is it now?'
   'Better, thanks. It's .... quite well.'

2   'Are Paula and Costas still going out together?'
   'No, they .... a couple of weeks ago.'

3   'Is it still cloudy outside?'
   'No, the weather's .... now. It's quite sunny.'

4   'Can you hear me?'
   'Not very well, it's noisy here. You'll have to .... !'

5   'Do you think he'll win the race?'
   'Only if he .... a lot in the last 400 metres.'

6   'Have you got any of that paint left?'
   'I'm afraid not. I .... it all .... doing the ceiling.'

5 Complete each sentence with the correct form, *a*, *b* or *c*.

1   I won't be going to the match on Saturday because I .... away on Friday.
   a   'll go
   b   'm going
   c   'll have been going

2   As soon as I hear the final score in the rugby, I .... you a text message.
   a   'm sending
   b   'll have sent
   c   'll send

3   It's a long way from here to the stadium. I .... you there if you like.
   a   'm driving
   b   'm going to drive
   c   'll drive

4   If you come to the athletics track at about 8 p.m. I .... in the 1500 metres, and you can cheer me on!
   a   'll be running
   b   'll run
   c   'm running

5   That player joined our club in the autumn, so by the end of the season he .... here for six months.
   a   'll have been playing
   b   'll be playing
   c   's going to be playing

6   We .... any idea who's playing in the match until the managers announce their teams.
   a   won't be having
   b   won't have
   c   aren't having

7   I'm sorry, but I can't go shopping with you on Saturday afternoon because I .... tennis.
   a   play
   b   'm playing
   c   'll play

8   If you carry on running around as fast as that, you .... all your energy by half time.
   a   're using up
   b   'll have been using up
   c   'll have used up

1 Replace the expressions in *italics* using phrases with these words and *in*. In some cases you need to add other words.

> course   doubt   favour   meantime
> mind   practice   progress   term

1 Please be quiet in the corridor. There's an examination *being done* in that room.

....

2 It's an expensive machine, but *over a long period of time* it may save the firm money.

....

3 It seemed a good idea to build a dam here, but *the real situation is that* it's harmed the local environment.

....

4 I *agree with the idea of* creating less waste in our everyday lives.

....

5 We cannot confirm your test scores yet, but you will be told *at a suitable time*.

....

6 The commercial success of the new aircraft is *not certain* given its high fuel consumption.

....

7 When companies close down factories, they should *think about* the effect on the workers.

....

8 My plane doesn't leave for another hour, so *from now until then* I'll do some shopping.

....

2 Complete the sentences using these words.

> contrast   despite   even   fact   hand
> nevertheless   spite   whereas

1 Studying science can be hard work. On the other .... , it can be very interesting.

2 They're going to build a huge new bridge, in .... of the enormous cost.

3 Some experiments take only a few seconds. In .... , others go on for years.

4 .... most cars use petrol, this one runs entirely on electricity.

5 People were walking on the ice, despite the .... that it was extremely thin.

6 There was thick fog at the airport. .... , some planes were taking off.

7 The new laptops are selling very well, ... though they are so expensive.

8 .... the terrible weather conditions, the team finally reached the South Pole.

3 Put the words in the correct order to form passive sentences.

1 tree / lightning / old / struck / the / by / was

....

....

2 should / sooner / repaired / been / the / have / damage

....

....

3 known / university / be / excellent / that / is / to

....

....

4 present / being / stadium / rebuilt / is / the / at

....

....

5 been / fire / carelessness / the / thought / have / to / caused / is / by

....

....

6 is / that / reduced / pollution / it / be / will / hoped

....

....

7 announced / government / been / policies / by / new / the / have

....

....

8 to / leaked / sea / believed / into / oil / have / is / the

....

....

4 Match the sentence halves using collocations as clues.

1 It's often cheaper to make long-distance
2 You just click here if you want to attach
3 In storms like this, the emergency
4 Before I buy anything online, I browse
5 The Olympics are seen by television
6 The Space Agency is planning to launch
7 In ten years, petrol will cost up to three
8 Scientists say they're going to carry out

a viewers across the world.
b a rocket carrying two astronauts into space.
c a few websites to compare prices.
d times as much as it does now.
e calls using a phone card.
f an experiment deep underground.
g a file to an email.
h services are always very busy.

5 Rewrite the sentences using *if*.

1 Without rain, plants don't grow.

2 I won't go out unless it stops raining.

3 I don't have enough money to buy a new laptop.

4 Fish can't live in this river because the water's so polluted.

5 I don't know Marta's phone number, so I can't call her.

6 I didn't wear boots because I didn't know the path would be so muddy.

7 We didn't take any food with us, so we were hungry.

8 I can find a job in Brazil because I studied Portuguese.

6 Find and correct sixteen mistakes with articles in the text below.

I really hate living in this cold part of the country in middle of winter. Sometimes, temperature drops to twenty degrees below the zero, and sun doesn't come up until nearly ten o'clock in the morning. I'm student, and I have to get out of the bed very early to catch earliest bus into the city so that I can get to school on time. Sometimes there is the heavy snow and bus is very late, or I have to stay at the home all day. That always seems to happen on the days when I have interesting lessons, for instance the chemistry, or music. I really enjoy playing piano. I wish I could live in a place that has the sunshine every day, like an island in Pacific Ocean, or city where it's always warm, such as Miami in United States.

Progress test 5 Units 9–10

1 Replace the words in *italics* with these extreme adjectives.

| absurd bizarre breathtaking delightful |
| dreadful ideal massive vivid |

1 When you first see the Himalayas, they are a *surprising* sight.

....

2 I love meeting famous people, so being a TV interviewer is *suitable* work for me.

....

3 A newspaper had a really *silly* story about a 1940s aeroplane being found on the moon!

....

4 It was a *very pleasant* programme about young animals in spring.

....

5 It's a *very big* media organisation, owning TV stations and newspapers around the world.

....

6 The *bright* colours of the flowers make this a beautiful scene.

....

7 Programmes about *very strange* things that have actually happened are very popular.

....

8 That's a *very bad* programme. I'm amazed anybody watches it.

....

2 Complete the sentences using nouns formed from these verbs with suitable suffixes.

| coincide explain entertain guide |
| intend promote produce vary |

1 Despite a lot of expensive ...., the film was not a commercial success.

2 As a young actor, I received some useful .... from established TV stars.

3 The film studio is working on a new .... of Shakespeare's play *Romeo and Juliet*.

4 Working in the .... industry, for example on TV or in films, can be great fun.

5 It was never my .... to become famous. Somehow it just seemed to happen.

6 You will have to give the police an .... of exactly what happened to the money.

7 It was a complete .... that my cousin and I both became celebrities in the same year.

8 There is a huge .... in prices here. Some clothes are cheap, and others cost a fortune.

3 Correct the mistakes in the verb forms.

1 I wish I earn more money in this job.

....

2 I missed the bus this morning. I wish I get up earlier.

....

3 I can't find my keys anywhere. I wish I can remember where I put them.

....

4 I wish I won't have to go to that meeting tomorrow.

....

5 If only I wasn't unkind to Rosa yesterday.

....

6 I really wish people stopped parking on the pavement. It's so annoying.

....

7 I wished I would have entered that talent show because I might have won.

....

8 If only I would sing a little bit better. I'd be a star!

....

4 Rewrite the words in *italics* using phrasal verbs with *out*.

1 When are you going to *put those horrible old clothes in the bin*?

....

2 I always like to *come home* late on Saturday nights.

....

3 *Draw a line through* any mistakes, then write the correct word above.

....

4 I took Alonso's new skateboard down the big hill to *see what it was like*.

....

5 Jane *left in a hurry* and forgot to close the front door.

....

6 If we don't go to the shop for more bread, we'll *have none left* soon.

....

7 The seller *changed his mind about* the agreement.

....

8 Dad's gone to bed because he's *extremely tired*.

....

5 Rewrite the sentences using the correct form of causative *have*.

1 While I waited, a nurse took my temperature.

....

....

2 Nobody's decorated our flat for many years.

....

....

3 I'm going to ask them to deliver the parcel later.

....

....

4 Someone stole my wallet while I was in the gym.

....

....

5 When you go through Airport Security, they'll take your photo.

....

....

6 I must ask someone to fix this washing machine.

....

....

7 I would've gone for a haircut if I'd had time.

....

....

8 They cut off the electricity because we hadn't paid the bills.

....

....

6 Complete the second sentence so that it means the same as the first sentence.

1 'I don't think you should spend so much money,' my friend said.

My friend advised ....

2 'I'm sorry I upset you yesterday,' Karen said to me.

Karen apologised ....

3 'Let's go shopping tomorrow,' Carmen said.

Carmen suggested ....

4 'I won't wear a tie with this jacket,' my brother said.

My brother refused ....

5 'Would you like to have dinner here this evening?' Daniel said to us.

Daniel invited ....

6 'Don't forget to bring your credit card,' my girlfriend said to me.

My girlfriend reminded ....

7 'I haven't told him what you said,' Helen said to me.

Helen denied ....

8 'I left all my money at home this morning,' said Mark.

Mark explained ....

Progress tests answer key

Progress test 1

1 1 d 2 e 3 a 4 b 5 f 6 c

2 1 Do you get 2 usually take 3 'm/am not going 4 'm/am getting 5 'm/am thinking 6 find 7 Does the boss know 8 're/are taking 9 arrives 10 's/is always criticising 11 don't deserve 12 doesn't surprise

3 1 competitive 2 greedy 3 dishonest 4 aggressive 5 energetic 6 foolish 7 emotional 8 unreliable 9 enthusiastic 10 unhelpful

4 1 was 2 told 3 had decided 4 had grown 5 went 6 used to spend 7 'd been going 8 had moved 9 missed 10 would send 11 was getting 12 'd been 13 'd begun 14 realised 15 'd moved

5 1 b 2 a 3 c 4 b 5 b 6 a 7 c 8 a

Progress test 2

1 1 popular with 2 capable of 3 ashamed of 4 supposed to 5 familiar with 6 prepared to 7 informed of 8 obsessed with

2 1 completely 2 extremely 3 quite 4 rather 5 a bit 6 quite 7 totally 8 absolutely 9 very 10 really

3 1 walking 2 spending 3 to go 4 to set off 5 to be 6 to get up 7 having 8 to get going 9 to have 10 doing 11 to wish 12 to bring 13 agreeing 14 sharing 15 to find 16 walking

4
1 Your brother is too young to travel on his own.
Your brother isn't old enough to travel on his own.
2 That team is too weak to win a single match.
That team isn't strong enough to win a single match.
3 It was too dark (for us) to see anything.
It wasn't light enough (for us) to see anything.
4 The hotel was too expensive for us to stay another night.
The hotel wasn't cheap/inexpensive enough for us to stay another night.
5 One runner was too slow to keep up with the others.
One runner wasn't fast/quick enough to keep up with the others.
6 Marion sang too badly to win a prize.
Marion didn't sing well enough to win a prize.

5 1 voyage 2 trip 3 hitchhiking 4 travel 5 expedition 6 hiking 7 tour 8 means

6 1 must have finished 2 might have been 3 can't have left 4 must have sold out 5 might have gone 6 can't have seen 7 must have snowed 8 might have been

Progress test 3

1 1 survivors 2 librarian 3 interviewee 4 servants 5 investors 6 electrician 7 trainer 8 physicist 9 attendants 10 manufacturers

2 1 when 2 who 3 which 4 – 5 that 6 which 7 where 8 who 9 when 10 that 11 which 12 whose 13 that 14 which 15 –

3 1 took up 2 take in 3 take out 4 taken over 5 taken off 6 take on 7 've taken to 8 take on

4 1 healing up 2 split up 3 clearing up *or* cleared up 4 speak up 5 speeds up 6 used … up

5 1 b 2 c 3 c 4 a 5 a 6 b 7 b 8 c

Progress test 4

1 1 in progress 2 in the long term 3 in practice 4 'm/am in favour of 5 in due course 6 in doubt 7 bear in mind 8 in the meantime

2 1 hand 2 spite 3 contrast 4 Whereas 5 fact 6 Nevertheless 7 even 8 Despite

3
1 The old tree was struck by lightning.
2 The damage should have been repaired sooner.
3 That university is known to be excellent.
4 The stadium is being rebuilt at present.
5 The fire is thought to have been caused by carelessness.
6 It is hoped that pollution will be reduced.
7 New policies have been announced by the government.
8 Oil is believed to have leaked into the sea.

4 1 e 2 g 3 h 4 c 5 a 6 b 7 d 8 f

5 1 If it doesn't rain, plants don't grow.

2 I won't go out if it doesn't stop raining.

3 If I had enough money, I'd / I would buy a new laptop.

4 Fish could live in this river if the water weren't/wasn't so polluted.

5 If I knew Marta's phone number, I could call her. (*or* I'd / I would call)

6 I would've / I would have worn boots if I'd / I had known the path would be so muddy.

7 If we'd / we had taken some food with us, we wouldn't / would not have been hungry.

8 I couldn't / I could not find a job in Brazil if I hadn't / had not studied Portuguese. (*or* wouldn't / would not be able to find)

(Reverse order of clauses also possible in 1–8.)

6 1 the middle   2 the temperature   3 below zero
4 the sun   5 a student   6 of bed   7 the earliest
8 there is heavy snow   9 the bus   10 at home
11 for instance chemistry   12 the piano
13 has sunshine   14 the Pacific Ocean
15 a city   16 the United States

Progress test 5

1 1 breathtaking   2 ideal   3 absurd   4 delightful
5 massive   6 vivid   7 bizarre   8 dreadful

2 1 promotion   2 guidance   3 production
4 entertainment   5 intention   6 explanation
7 coincidence   8 variation

3 1 wish I earned   2 wish I'd / I had got up (*or* could get up)
3 wish I could remember   4 wish I didn't have to
5 If only I hadn't been
6 wish people would stop parking (*or* would not / wouldn't park)
7 I wished I'd / I had entered   8 If only I could sing

4 1 throw out those old clothes *or* throw those old clothes out
2 stay out   3 Cross out   4 try it out   5 rushed out
6 run out   7 backed out of   8 worn out

5 1 While I waited, I had my temperature taken (by a nurse).

2 We haven't had our flat decorated for many years.

3 I'm going to have the parcel delivered later.

4 I had my wallet stolen while I was in the gym.

5 When you go through Airport Security, you'll have your photo taken.

6 I must have this washing machine fixed.

7 I would've had my hair cut if I'd had time.

8 We had the electricity cut off because we hadn't paid the bills.

6 1 me not to spend so much money.

2 for upsetting me the previous day. (*or* the day before)

3 going shopping *or* (that) we should go shopping the next day. (*or* the day after, the following day)

4 to wear a tie with that jacket.

5 us to have dinner there that evening. (*or* in the evening)

6 me to bring my credit card.

7 telling him what I'd / I had said. (*or* that she had told him.)

8 (that) he'd / he had left all his money at home that morning. (*or* in the morning)

Author Acknowledgements

The author would like to thank Neil Holloway and Liz Driscoll for all their input, efficiency and good humour. Many thanks to Matt Stephens (production project manager), Chloe Szebrat (permissions controller), Alison Prior (picture researcher), Leon Chambers (audio producer), Alicia McAuley (proof reader).

Publisher acknowledgements

Development of this publication has made use of the Cambridge English Corpus (CEC). The CEC is a computer database of contemporary spoken and written English, which currently stands at over one billion words. It includes British English, American English and other varieties of English. It also includes the Cambridge Learner Corpus, developed in collaboration with the University of Cambridge ESOL Examinations. Cambridge University Press has built up the CEC to provide evidence about language use that helps to produce better language teaching materials.

This product is informed by the English Vocabulary Profile, built as part of English Profile, a collaborative programme designed to enhance the learning, teaching and assessment of English worldwide. Its main funding partners are Cambridge University Press and Cambridge ESOL and its aim is to create a 'profile' for English linked to the Common European Framework of Reference for Languages (CEF). English Profile outcomes, such as the English Vocabulary Profile, will provide detailed information about the language that learners can be expected to demonstrate at each CEF level, offering a clear benchmark for learners' proficiency. For more information, please visit www.englishprofle.org

The Cambridge Advanced Learner's Dictionary is the world's most widely used dictionary for learners of English. Including all the words and phrases that learners are likely to come across, it also has easy-to-understand definitions and example sentences to show how the word is used in context. The Cambridge Advanced Learner's Dictionary is available online at dictionary.cambridge.org. © Cambridge University Press, Third edition (2008), reproduced with permission.